ASCENT
OF THE
A-WORD

Geoffrey Nunberg

ASCENT
OF THE
A-WORD

Assholism,
the First Sixty Years

PublicAffairs

New York

Published in the United States by PublicAffairs™,
a Member of the Perseus Books Group

Printed in the United States of America.

PublicAffairs books are available at special discounts for bulk purchases in the
U.S. by corporations, institutions, and other organizations. For more information,
please contact the Special Markets Department at the Perseus Books Group,
2300 Chestnut Street, Suite 200, Philadelphia, PA 19103, call (800) 810-4145,
ext. 5000, or e-mail special.markets@perseusbooks.com.

Library of Congress Cataloging-in-Publication Data
Nunberg, Geoffrey, 1945–
The ascent of the A-word : assholism, the first sixty years / Geoffrey Nunberg.
    p.   cm.
Includes index.
ISBN 978-1-61039-175-7 (hardcover) — ISBN 978-1-61039-176-4 (electronic)
    1. English language—Obscene words. 2. Words, Obscene. I. Title.
PE3724.O3N86   2012
427—dc23

                                                                    2012017027

Editorial production by *Marra*thon Production Services. www.marrathon.net

BOOK DESIGN BY JANE RAESE
Text set in 12-point Bembo

FIRST EDITION

10 9 8 7 6 5 4 3 2 1

Contents

Introduction

The sun shineth upon the dunghill and is not corrupted.
—John Lyly, *Euphues*, 1578

When Barbara Walters announced the 2011 version of her annual list of the Ten Most Fascinating People, it was headed by Steve Jobs and included Donald Trump, Simon Cowell, Herman Cain, and the Kardashians, along with Derek Jeter, Katy Perry, Amanda Knox, Pippa Middleton, and the actors who play the two gay guys on *Modern Family*. I make that five out of ten who are assholes (I'm giving Jeter a pass because he's a gamer and passing over the reports about his sending his one-night stands home in a limo with a basket of autographed gear). However you reckon it, it was a banner year for high-profile assholes, and if Walters hadn't been particular about interviewing her choices (the living ones, anyway), she could have easily filled all ten places several times over with other members of the breed. She left out Charlie Sheen, whose drug-addled meltdown in early 2011 so captured the nation's attention—he was briefly adding more than a hundred thousand Twitter followers a day—that he took it on the road in a national tour. She could have added Hank Williams Jr., who made news when he compared Obama to Hitler, Dominique Strauss-Kahn, Silvio Berlusconi, and John Galliano (Hitler again). There could have been slots for Reps. Anthony Weiner, D-NY (lascivious tweets) and Christopher Lee, R-NY

(Craigslist trolling). And Walters left out Newt Gingrich, whose presidential campaign unexpectedly caught fire for a while when, having bailed on Trump and Cain, Republicans decided they could overlook his being an asshole to his previous wives because he promised to be just the asshole who could take it to Obama good.

Yet 2011 wasn't exceptional in that line. Over the years, Walters' lists have included a remarkable number of names that are regularly paired with the asshole label: Rush Limbaugh, Tiger Woods, Tom Cruise, LeBron James, Karl Rove, and Sarah Palin (all of whom, along with Trump, made the list twice or more), as well as Jerry Springer, Sumner Redstone, Mark Zuckerberg, Bret Favre, James Cameron, Kate Gosselin, Glenn Beck, Michael Moore, the Jersey Shore kids, "Dr. Phil" McGraw, Mel Gibson, Curt Schilling, Kanye West, Don Imus, Hugo Chavez, Dennis Rodman, Rupert Murdoch, Benjamin Netanyahu, Martha Stewart, and Andre Agassi. Some of those calls may be arguable, and there are other names on Walters' lists that some people would assign to the category, like Nancy Pelosi, Mark McGwire, Hillary Clinton, and Arnold Schwarzenegger. But whatever adjustments you make, it's clear that Walters hasn't had to tip the scales. Assholes may constitute only a small proportion of the figures in public life, but they get a big share of the ink and pixels.

What is it that draws us to these people? There's no one answer. Some of it is just the age-old fascination with Celebrities Behaving Badly, compounded by the ubiquity of technology for capturing and broadcasting their misbehavior and the media's eagerness to share the details with us. There are assholes who simultaneously intrigue and appall us, like

Sheen, Galliano, and Gibson, whose outbursts reveal streaks of hatefulness or unchecked egomania. Some of it answers to the no less eternal satisfaction of watching combat and confrontation, as performed by the barking heads on what Deborah Tannen calls the "let's you and him fight" genre of talk shows, or more recently, on politically monochromatic programming dominated by a single resident bully like Bill O'Reilly. Some assholes titillate us with their effrontery, like Omarosa, Richard Hatch, and the other reality show manipulators who become celebrities in their own right. And still others suggest the undeniable allure of people who are in a position to indulge the undiluted whims of ego or vent their anger and contempt without concern for the proprieties—cultural rock stars like Kanye West and Steve Jobs, who act like assholes because they can.

The visibility of these icons of assholism isn't necessarily evidence for the collapse of civility and the coarsening of public life, much less for a general deterioration of national character. However dire things may seem, on the whole we're as nice as we ever were, particularly in the way we treat our friends, family, and colleagues. In some ways we're a good deal nicer. But indisputably there's an intense interest in the asshole phenomenon. Every age creates a particular social offender that it makes a collective preoccupation—the cad in Anthony Trollope's day, the phony that Holden Caulfield was fixated on in the postwar years—and the asshole is ours. In fact you could argue that some of those archetypes play a cathartic role for us: Donald Trump acts like an asshole so we don't have to. But the preoccupation also reflects the modern creation of new and unprecedented settings for acting like assholes, in both public and private life, opening the way to varieties of behavior that people a few generations ago would have found not so much shocking as weird: think of the varieties of digital miscreants denominated lurkers, cyberstalkers, sock puppets, and blog trolls. This isn't entirely a deplorable development, or at least you can see it as the collateral consequence of some healthy ones. The advent of the asshole is a reflex of very sweeping revisions in the personal and social values that we all share, even if we sometimes find ourselves railing about them. The point of this book, more than anything else, is that the ascent of the A-word and the attention it gets say a great deal about who we've become.

. . .

Asshole is always a disreputable word, whether it's referring to someone's anatomy or his character. But it's only the latter use of the word that can move people to laughter. That was invariably people's reaction when I answered their question about what I was working on by telling them it was a book about assholes. That response made me a little defensive, and my questioner was often obliged to listen to an unbidden disquisition about why the topic was actually worthy of attention. But it was also reassuring to know how many people find it amusing that someone would want to write a serious book about such a topic. The words that make us laugh aren't usually ones we give a great deal of thought to. To study *asshole* is to dip into a pool unrippled by deep contemplation, insulated from the airs and distension that can infect a word like *incivility*, which provides an accurate reflection of what we genuinely think about how we should behave toward one another.

As my subtitle suggests, I'm really interested not in assholes so much as assholism, along with its close relation assholery. The English language isn't as accommodating here as some other languages, which have standard words for the things that assholes do, like the Spanish *pendejada*, from *pendejo* (literally a pubic hair), and the Italian *stronzata*, from *stronzo* (turd). English is an adaptable language, of course, and it isn't hard to find instances of *assholery* going back forty years in the works of writers like Thomas Pynchon and John Irving. But dictionaries haven't yet acknowledged the term (a telling diffidence, in this day and age, when the *Oxford English Dictionary* is at pains to demonstrate its hipness by including items like *wassup* and *BFF*). And while speakers of other languages seem more disposed to talk about *pendejismo, stronzismo,* or *Arschlochismus*—Europeans have a penchant for isms—English hasn't opened its arms to *assholism*, either, though the word made its first print appearance more than forty years ago in an essay by the Beat writer Seymour Krim. But "recognized word" or no, I need *assholism* here, because what I'm interested in isn't a distinct species of congenital jerks, but a social condition and a disposition that everyone is liable to on trying occasions. In fact I toyed with the idea of writing the book without citing any names at all, just to make the point, but as you've already seen, that idea didn't last long.

This is also a book about the word *asshole,* its true, but chiefly because of what it conveys. There are some vulgar and obscene words that are compelling in their own right. *Fuck* is the quintessential taboo word of English in all its uses, literal and figurative, as verb, intensifier, interjection, the focus of a long history of controversy and litigation. As a word alone, it's worthy of the book-length treatment that the lexicographer Jesse Sheidlower gives it in *The F-Word*. But *asshole* is of linguistic interest only so far as it colors the concept it names. True, it isn't purely by historical accident that *asshole* came to denote assholes and *prick* came to denote pricks (though the connection is obvious only after the fact—*prick* was once a term of endearment, and when *asshole* first appeared in GI slang during World War II, some people thought it meant something like *nerd*). But there are a lot of other words that people use to more or less the same effect. It's in the nature of slang to churn out mutations and variants, and *asshole* has more than its share. The word was just a few years old when *ass wipe* appeared (it made its first print appearance in 1952 in Saul Bellow's *The Adventures of Augie March*), and over the years it has been joined by *asshat*, *assclown*, and *assbag*, among others, while unrelated items like *douchebag, dipshit*, and *dickhead* circulate in the same semantic neighborhood.

In language as elsewhere, we don't like the idea of a difference without a distinction, and you can find people who will explain the subtle points that distinguish an asshole from an assclown or a douchebag, though usually without much precision or consistency (actually, dictionaries don't do any better with these). But despite the variation, everyone recognizes *asshole* as the primary name of a basic category of American moral life. People agree about prototypical cases like this one (which was actually witnessed by someone I know):

On Sept. 11, 2001, with all flights cancelled across the country, you're in the Hertz rental agency in Manhattan, trying desperately to rent a car to get home to your family in Texas, along with a large crowd of anxious people trying to do the same thing. A man walks in, pushes to the front of the crowd, and asks the clerk, "Where's the Hertz Gold Card line?" You turn to your friend standing next to you and say, "What a(n) _____!"

That was one of the questions I put on a brief questionnaire that I gave to a few dozen people, speakers of English and other languages, asking them to give me the vulgar word that best fit the situation. Among the Americans and Canadians who answered, ranging in age from twenty to sixty-eight, almost all said "asshole," apart from two who offered "douchebag." You wouldn't call it science, but it was close enough to confirm that most people classify that sort of person in the same way. The agreement was almost that general when the question was:

A policeman stops a motorist for speeding. The motorist, a well-dressed man, says, "I'm a lawyer and I'm late for an important court date. Wouldn't your time be better spent arresting real criminals?" What word(s) would you expect the police officer to use to describe the motorist to his fellow officers?

But they reacted differently to another example:

"Eddie tricked his partner Larry into putting the firm's accounts in his own name, then let Larry take the blame when the fraud was discovered by the authorities. What a(n) _____!"

Here the answers ran to *shit* and *bastard*, with only one person offering *asshole* and nobody offering *douche*. So the respondents more or less agreed that the first two belong to the same category and third to a different one. True, you wouldn't expect to see the kind of uniformity here that you would if you asked people about the difference between chairs and sofas, say. That's partly because of linguistic variation (a lot of people don't have *douchebag* in their vocabularies at all, particularly women) and partly because we subdivide the moral landscape in somewhat different ways. Still, when we hear Clint Eastwood or Woody Allen describing somebody as an asshole, we all have a pretty clear idea of what he's saying.*

The level of agreement obviously falls off once we leave the North American continent. The British have the same word, or rather *arsehole*, but it shares its semantic space with a family of native-grown epithets like *tosser*, *wanker*, and *git*, not to mention the C-word, which is much less shocking to British ears than to American when it's used for an obnoxious man. (Some of the British speakers I asked about those examples favored *wanker* for the Hertz example, though some offered *arsehole* as well.) Even so, it's fair to say the British and Australians recognize the asshole as a type—they're quite clear about what Eastwood and Allen are saying, too. And *asshole* has equivalents, if not exact synonyms, in other Western lan-

---

*Some people seem to use *asshole* as an all-purpose word of condemnation. I've seen it applied to Hitler and Pol Pot, for example. I think that occludes some significant moral distinctions, to put it mildly, but if you're of the opinion that those people are best described as assholes, then we're using the word differently—or maybe we're just using different words.

guages—French *connard*, Dutch *klootsak*, German *Arschloch*, Italian *stronzo*, and Spanish *pendejo, boludo*, or *gillipollas*, depending on the region. Each of them has its quirks, but if you know what an asshole is you're going to get *stronzo* and *Arschloch* right at least 90 percent of the time. It would be absurd to suggest that all those peoples organize their notions of appropriate social behavior along the exact same lines that Americans do. But when that asshole appears at the Hertz counter waving his gold card we can all roll our eyes at each other with a reasonable confidence that we're thinking pretty much the same thing. So while I'm looking only at American language and American attitudes in this book, I think a fair amount of it applies to other places that have undergone a lot of the same modern experience.

• • •

Considering how often the word *asshole* appears in the book, I can see where it may seem a little coy to have referred to it on the cover only as the A-word and in the derived form *assholism*—all the more since titles with vulgar words are so *du jour* right now. Not long ago, the *Times Literary Supplement* (*TLS*) columnist "J.C." (James Campbell) took a passing shot at what he called "the blood-draining horror of mainstream Christmas fare (*Do Ants Have Arseholes?*, *My Shit Life So Far*, etc.)." He could have pointed as well to recent American titles like *Sh*t My Dad Says*, *Go the F*ck to Sleep*, and *If You Give a Kid a Cookie, Will He Shut the F**k Up? Asshole* has gotten a lot of work in this line, too. The Stanford Business School professor Robert Sutton had a business bestseller a couple of years ago with *The No Asshole Rule,* and the "advice, how-to, and miscellaneous" shelf features entries such as *A Is for Asshole: The Grownups' ABC's of Conflict Resolution; Dear Asshole* ("101 Tear-Out Letters to the Morons who Muck up Your Life"); *A$$hole* ("How I Got Rich and Happy by Not Giving a Damn about Anyone and How You Can, Too); and *A**hole No More* ("A self-help guide for recovering a**holes and their victims"). There are lad-lit books like *The Complete A**hole's Guide to Handling Chicks*, complemented by monitory lass-lit titles like *Let's Face It, Men Are @$$#%\$* and *Are All Guys Assholes?* And in a class by itself—and my favorite of any genre—is a zombie parody called *Night of the Assholes*, by Kevin L. Donihe, the plot of which turns on the premise that people who treat assholes in an asshole way turn into assholes themselves, which in a way is the point of this book, too.

I don't find any of this quite as blood-draining as the *TLS's* Campbell does, but even so I had reservations about using the bare word *asshole* in the title. I suppose I could have appealed to the dispensation that allows disinterested scholars to address indelicate matters without impropriety, to touch pitch and not be defiled. But it doesn't quite work like that. Vulgar words like these tend to bleed through quotation marks; they jerk and quiver even on the dissection table. Most of us aren't troubled about seeing them in the printed pages of a book, which involves a quiet conversation between us and the author (anyone who does find it disturbing presumably hasn't gotten this far). But even in a linguistics class, I prefer not to say them aloud if I can avoid it, since that's sure to evoke either tittering, or more often, the sound of people audibly not tittering. And on the cover of a book, before the compact between author and reader is sealed—well, it isn't quite the same as wearing a T-shirt that says "Instant Asshole, Just Add Alcohol," but it's hard to argue that it isn't being partly done for effect. Often that's entirely defensible: What else would you call a parody about zombie assholes, *Night of the Vulgarians*? And in a very different way, I imagine that when the philosopher Harry Frankfurt wrote the engaging essay "On Bullshit" (which appeared in the *Raritan Review* before it was published as a book in 2005), the title was intended to make the point that the importance of bullshit to the theory of truth ought to make the vulgarity of its word irrelevant. But I don't think for a moment that the vulgarity of *asshole* is incidental to its meaning (actually, I don't think the vulgarity of *bullshit* is, either). I take it very seriously, as something central to the work the word does for us, for better and for worse. If *asshole* weren't crude, we'd have to find something else to call the guy who's yelling at the harassed airport gate agent about his upgrade. So if I dance around the word in the title of this book, you could think of it as an homage to its power. Considering all it does for us, and to us, *asshole* doesn't get nearly the respect it deserves.

chapter one

The Word

So long as I regard stupidity as a news item, a misfortune that happens only to others, or to me only under an outside influence—I wasn't myself, I can't think what happened to me—the subtlety of the phenomenon eludes me.
—André Glucksmann, *La Bêtise,* 1986

Assholes and Anti-assholes

The idea that *asshole* could be a proxy for the fraying fabric of public life first struck me in 2005, just before things got really squirrelly. I was writing about the language of politics and listening to a lot of right-wing talk on radio and TV and I kept noticing how everything seemed to be aimed at depicting liberals as, well, assholes. Not that anyone ever actually says *assholes* on the air on the programs, bleeped or not.* But that isn't the point; it's rather that *asshole* seems to encapsulate

---

*To my knowledge, the word has been used only once on Fox News, by an AFL-CIO economist who lost it with the host Neil Cavuto when Cavuto asked him if he had gotten his degree at a baking school—which to be sure really was kind of an asshole thing to say.

I

the animus the shows are both stoking and stroking. It's a word we reserve for members of our own tribe: the boss who takes credit for your work, the neighbors who get on your case for putting out your garbage the night before, or maybe a well-known politician or celebrity. It isn't a word you'd use of Abu Musab al-Zarqawi. It signals indignation, with an undercurrent of contempt, an emotion you can only feel towards those you feel both superior to and familiar with. And that feeling in turn legitimates a certain energizing response— combative, derisory, with more than a splash of asshole itself—that's compelling enough to keep listeners tuned in, which is after all the aim of the exercise. Or if the listeners are of an opposing political viewpoint, as many of them are, they can enjoy a rush of head-clearing rage at the hosts' assholistic harangues. Assholes are people who allow us to be assholes back at them. They turn us into anti-assholes, a word I think of as being less like antitoxin than antimatter—stuff just like matter but of an opposite charge, which reacts with matter violently.

A huge amount of this programming is aimed at creating exchanges and narratives that generate these feelings by turning reports about remote evils into pretexts for stirring up more intimate antipathies. During the buildup to the Iraq war, more than half the Fox News segments on Iraq focused on the pusillanimity of the French, who were refusing to go along with the invasion, and through them, on the pretentious American Francophile liberals who spoke their language and consumed their wines and cheese. (The Germans, who were no less adamantly opposed to the invasion, got a pass.) Saddam Hussein may have been an oriental despot out of central casting, but he was too alien to be the object of the contempt that only familiarity can breed.

Not that conservatives always had to manufacture such pretexts. You can't live in San Francisco and teach at Berkeley, as I do, without being impressed by the myriad forms of assholism that bourgeois liberals nourish: the pretension and superiority, the preciosity, the way laudable commitments to social justice sit cheek by jowl with intrusive paternalism. (Berkeley has always been a place where people believe that consenting adults should be allowed to do whatever they please in the privacy of their bedroom so long as they don't try to smoke afterwards.) The truth is that the dynamic I'm interested in here—the play of asshole and anti-asshole—is fed by the abundant strains of assholism that run through every corner of American life. What struck me in 2005 was the way the play of asshole and anti-asshole was bubbling up into the public sphere, like a sadistic form of performance art or a snarky sitcom.

• • •

That was seven years ago, in what in retrospect seems almost an idyllic age of comity, before public discourse started to go completely off the rails. The most dramatic shift was among the partisans of the right, who discovered after Barack Obama's election just how gratifying it could be to act like an asshole when you could tell yourself you had a sufficient provocation and were unencumbered by the responsibilities of government. In an emblematic case, the first-term South Carolina congressman Joe Wilson interrupted a presidential speech on the health care bill to call out, "You lie!" The conduct was deemed unbecoming by his own party's leadership—"totally disrespectful," said John McCain—and Wilson initially apologized and said he had let his emotions get the better of him. But radio hosts celebrated his "guts" and "backbone" and said he had no need to apologize for simply articulating what millions of Americans were saying. Supporters flooded Wilson with campaign contributions, and a bit more alarmingly, a South Carolina gun dealer offered a limited edition component for the AR-15 with "You Lie" etched on the stock, as if acting like an asshole provided incontrovertible proof of patriotic zeal.

This didn't come out of nowhere. Fifty years ago, the historian and traditionalist conservative Peter Viereck, recalling the humanism of Burke and Adams, wrote that modern conservatism was diffusing a mood of emotional freeze, making people "ashamed of generous social impulses." And in modern times, the right has always been susceptible to making an exhibition of its hardheartedness, just as the left has had a regrettable penchant for self-congratulatory pietism. But lately the tone of those displays has become more intense and operatic, as witness the striking series of outbursts during the debates among Republican presidential hopefuls in 2011–2012. A debate audience applauded when Brian Williams began a question to Governor Rick Perry by noting that Texas has conducted a record 234 executions during his term as governor, then booed Perry himself when he defended a Texas program providing in-state college tuition to the children of undocumented immigrants. (In his defense, Perry said, "If you say that we should not educate children who have come into our state . . . by no fault of their own, I don't think you have a heart"—a remark that so angered right-wing voters that Perry was placed in the situation, surely unprecedented in American politics, of having to apologize for using the "inappropriate" word *heart*.) In another debate, the audience booed a gay soldier serving in Iraq who asked in a clip what Rick Santorum would do about "Don't Ask, Don't Tell." A debate audience cheered Herman Cain's assertion that "if you don't have a job and you're not rich, blame yourself." And at a CNN–Tea Party debate, Wolf Blitzer asked Ron Paul what should happen to a person who lacks health insurance and falls into a coma. "Are you saying that society should just let him die?" Blitzer asked, at which point several people yelled, "Yeah!" and others cheered. By early 2012, a South Carolina debate audience was moved to boo Paul when he said that other countries didn't like being bombed any more than we would, adding, "I would say that maybe we ought to consider a Golden Rule in foreign policy." The audience's reservations about Paul's proposal may have been soundly rooted in *Realpolitik*, but even so it was a theologically awkward moment. If you took those effusions at face value, they seemed to confirm the continued relevance of Viereck's observation that among a slice of modern conservatives, it's cool to be cruel.

It's misleading to judge any group by its most demonstrative adherents. Wilson was plainly out of line even by the standards of his caucus, and the audiences at primary season debates—candidates' supporters provided with tickets by the campaigns and urged by the producers to be demonstrative—were clearly more vociferous than the typical adherent of the Tea Party right, the conservative movement, or the Republican Party in general. Still, the groundswell of support for the outbursts suggests that these attitudes are widespread. And yet these people are neither demented extremists nor political neo-phytes: they're people who were mad at Gore, mad at Clinton, mad at Carter. This isn't a new constituency in American pol-itics, just an old one steamed over. So what has gotten into them? People point to race as a motivation, and there's clearly something to that: it's sobering how many of the online com-ments about Obama and the Democrats at conservative sites manage to work in references to affirmative action, water-melons, Chicago thugs, and Kenya. But few deserve the labels of "terrorists" or "crazies" that critics on the left have thrown at them, and notwithstanding the occasional demonstrator holding a sign that depicts Obama as a witch doctor with a bone through his nose, the majority weren't driven to their participation by virulent racist attitudes. Indeed, you have the sense that a fair amount of their race talk is just the collateral effect of a free-floating outrage that will seize opportunisti-cally on any inimical attribute that comes to hand. When it comes to the crunch, there isn't that much difference in tone between their vilifications of the Muslim Kenyan socialist America-hating Barack Hussein Obama for being so exceed-ingly Other and their vilifications of Bill Clinton for being so exceedingly anything but, as web comments indicate:

Wanna talk about the country's "First Black President"? Hell, he was a hick-ass bubba long before he went black: worthless, shiftless, non-productive, lazy, no account, philandering piece of poor white trash.

• • •

That intensified tone of vituperation isn't the direct result of a shift to more hardline political attitudes. Not that there hasn't been one, but it itself is largely the outgrowth of a change in political style. Michael Tomasky has argued that the character of the new right was shaped more by rhetoric than by ideas:

> Usually a political movement is driven by its ideas. Then it chooses the rhetoric it thinks best advances the ideas. I've long thought that sometime in the 1990s, this normal process reversed itself on the American right, and rhetoric began driving, and even elbowing out, ideas. Once this wall is breached, compromise on any important issue becomes impossible, and responsible policymaking nearly so.

There's no question rhetoric has become one of the principal drivers of the politics of the right. But the word itself may be misleading. These days it usually has a narrow sense; say "rhetoric," and what comes to mind is the use of emotionally charged words ("traditional values," "reproductive freedom") and tendentious metaphors and comparisons ("death taxes," the economy as a family budget)—words that call up pictures in people's heads and dispose them to think in a certain way. But rhetoric is also a matter of making connections, of arranging the conversation so that the listeners feel a sense of community with the speaker and with each other. And the "conservative rhetoric factory," as Tomasky calls it, promulgates not just a vocabulary but a tone, an ethos, a way of presenting oneself in relation to the other side. What makes Rush Limbaugh so adept a rhetorician isn't so much the words he uses or the comparisons he makes as the attitude he conveys and the sympathetic chords he strikes with and between his listeners. The asshole/anti-asshole business isn't the only maneuver that works this end, but it is central to the way a lot of people construe their political identity—to what it actually means to be a "conservative" or a "liberal." The web is full of ads for T-shirts that say "I'm everything the liberals hate" or "I'm every conservative's worst nightmare," and in fact that's how a lot of partisans think of themselves, as in the business of infuriating the assholes on the other side.

That dynamic explains the oddly insouciant hardheartedness of those debate outbursts. I say "oddly" because these people aren't constitutionally cruel or sadistic. In the *New York Review of Books*, Charles Simic described the 2011 Republican debates as "celebrations of meanness and inhumanity." But in fact the animus here is only incidentally directed at the actual victims of the controversial policies—the executed convicts, the gay soldiers, the hapless uninsured, or the child of undocumented immigrants who was brought into the country at five and wants to go to college to become a veterinarian. True, those people are dehumanized, which is always a prerequisite for a tactical unfeelingness. (What could be more dehumanizing than the noun *illegals*, a term that reduces people to their infractions?) As Rick Perry observed to his detriment, it's only by suppressing your reflexive compassion that you can oppose providing college tuition for that undocumented teenager, which is otherwise as close to a moral and economic no-brainer as any issue in American political life.

But for just that reason, those victims themselves aren't satisfying objects of contempt. You may be indignant about the law-breaking aliens who are flooding across our borders, but you aren't apt to think of them as assholes or lie awake fuming about them in the middle of the night, the way you do about an insufferable co-worker or cousin. True hatred and contempt are more intimate emotions than that. The real targets of the aggression here are the liberal bleeding hearts who favor amnesty for illegal aliens, the same people who support the radical homosexual agenda, the government takeover of health care, and gay marriage. The more outrageous and callous the position you take on those issues, the greater the pleasure in imagining the conniptions it will give to the other side, and the greater the sense of camaraderie you create with your fellows. It's the political equivalent of smut, as Freud explained the notion, like the men in a tavern who make salacious jokes when the barmaid enters the room in order to enjoy her discomfort at their displaced aggression.★ Think of Ann Coulter saying that the 9/11 widows enjoyed their husbands' deaths. The remark was flamboyantly cruel and tasteless, but it wasn't personal; Coulter couldn't care less about those women one way or another. But it came off as sufficiently monstrous to rouse liberals to steaming indignation— "Heartless!" said Hillary Clinton, as if on cue—and by the by to get Coulter invited to *The Today Show* to repeat the remark

---

★Rush Limbaugh managed to achieve a fusion of the two forms of smut in his remarks in March 2012 about Sandra Fluke, the Georgetown Law student who had testified to a Democratic group for the need for easier access to birth control. Fluke, he said, "essentially says that she must be paid to have sex, what does that make her? It makes her a slut, right? It makes her a prostitute." But aimed as it was at a civilian, the charge was too personal for many, including a number of Limbaugh's advertisers, and reeked a little too much of the tavern.

for the delectation of viewers, outraging some to the delight of some others.

People talking about the polarization of American political life often speak of "demonization" of the other side—a recondite theological term before it suddenly became popular in the mid-1980s. But demonization is too broad a notion to be very helpful. You can demonize anyone from the Jews to the oil companies to Tiger Woods to PC users, but the color and intensity of the animus is different in each case. What's going on here is much more specific. It's assholization: the more of an asshole you can make your adversaries seem, the more of an asshole you can permit yourself to appear, so as to bond with your fellows with provocative gestures of insensitivity, real or, very often, fantasized, as various web comments reveal:

> Next time you're in line waiting behind that welfare moocher, don't forget to yell out "You're Welcome" as they walk away from the register with all that crap you just bought for them. Trust me, the look they will give you is worth it. If your lucky, they'll smart off at you which will be your invitation to further humiliate their sorry ass. Yea, I know, I'm being insensitive. Cry me a freakin river.

> Saturday I was parked in a shopping center. When I returned to my car I had difficulty getting into my driver's door because the a-hole next to me had parked waaay too close. I tried very hard not to scratch their car door getting in, but then I noticed their Obama bumper stickers. Oh, well. Accidents happen.

> I was driving south on the Meadowbrook on LI. This guy
> was stuck in the left lane with his hood up. I was slowing
> down to help him and then I saw a big Bush/Cheney 2004
> sticker. I sped up and left. I don't feel particularly bad about
> it. He would have gotten fat and lazy if I helped him.

This is a fairly pointed maneuver, which by no means covers every variety of political stupidity, belligerence, or malice. You aren't necessarily an asshole for asserting that Obama is a Muslim born in Kenya. Nor for that matter are you an asshole for holding that Bush and Cheney were responsible for 9/11 or that global warming is a hoax perpetrated by a cabal of greedy scientists. But you might be an asshole if you asserted those things not because you believe them but because they're the sort of thing that pisses off people on the other side.

It's assholism if people take some pleasure in justifying it with the proposition, "It's impolite (cruel, unfair), yeah, but the asshole has it coming." Joe Wilson's defenders didn't deny that his outburst was intemperate, but rather stressed the provocation; he was "Rude but Right," as *National Review* headed the story. And not even the most devoted fans of O'Reilly or Limbaugh would deny that they traffic in contention or suggest that they're basically sweet and easygoing guys; they'll say that it's no more than those liberal assholes deserve. Anyway, they say, the other side does the same thing. They're right about that, too. Conservatives may have had more success with belligerent broadcast formats, but liberals haven't eschewed opportunities for playing the anti-asshole to the assholes on the right. Michael Moore has built a whole career around the maneuver, and the hosts on MSNBC have been known to go there, too.

(I think of Chris Matthews interviewing Michele Bachmann remotely at her campaign headquarters after her congressional election victory in 2010. "Are you hypnotized?" he asked her, after she kept ducking a question about Republican plans, while Keith Olbermann sniggered in the background.) And if you were looking for examples of flamboyant assholism among political demonstrators, you'd be hard put to beat the antics of some of the anti-war protestors in San Francisco back in February of 2003, who took the marching cry of "no business as usual" as justification for blocking traffic and leaving commuters stuck in their cars for hours, not to mention the "Pukers for Peace" who vomited on the steps of the Federal Building to demonstrate that they were sick of war. ("There's nothing like this in Phoenix," the *San Francisco Chronicle* reported one Arizona tourist as saying.) There were similar gestures at some of the Occupy venues in 2011 and 2012, mostly from Black Bloc "anarchists" like the ones who smashed windows and slashed tires along Valencia Street in my own San Francisco Mission neighborhood on the eve of May 1, 2012, having redirected their rage at the 1 percent toward the "bougies" whose cars and coffeehouses were more conveniently at hand. The rhetorical strategy was almost identical to that of the right. If the Tea Party made everything about the asshole liberals, the anarchists made everything about the asshole yuppies. It comes to pretty much the same thing. The difference, over and above the violence of the latter, is that the anarchists are a marginal if troubling element in the Occupy movement, whereas the assholism of the right is far more extensive and coherent at every level—not because conservatives are bigger assholes than liberals, but because they're much better organized about it.

Still, the same broad attitudes are coming into play, and not just in the realm of politics. These asshole/anti-asshole exchanges pervade our discussions of manners and mores, of technology, of finance, of birdwatching (really), of grammar.★ They've even become common on sports talk radio, which I had always thought of as the one island of public discourse where hosts and callers are generally committed to civility and mutual respect. It sometimes seems as if every corner of our public discourse is riddled with people depicting one another as assholes and treating them accordingly, whether or not they actually use the word.

No Ordinary Rudeness

People who find this sort of thing troubling—and almost everyone does, though selectively—tend to file it under the capacious heading of the decline of civility in public life. Yet there's nothing new about a contentious political climate. As historians keep pointing out, American politics has a long tradition of vituperation, invective, and even violence. Whatever

---

★ Public criticisms of someone's grammar have almost always involved assholism, long before there was a name for it. The point was taken to absurdity in a contribution by Alexander Nazaryan to the *New York Daily News* book blog that criticized the sloppy grammar and punctuation in the website of Trayvon Martin's killer George Zimmerman: "Zimmerman is accused of being a careless vigilante who played fast and loose with the law; why would he want to give credence to that argument by playing fast and loose with the most basic laws of grammar?" But the absurdity is only slightly diminished when someone takes the grammatical slips of Dwight Eisenhower or George W. Bush as evidence for his incompetence.

abuse critics have heaped on Bush or Obama doesn't have a patch on the things people were saying in the 1864 election, when the Democrats called Lincoln a leering buffoon and Horace Greeley accused the Democrats of stealing the votes of dead Union soldiers. Opponents were no less brutal about the Roosevelts in the 1930s (kids were still repeating Eleanor Roosevelt jokes when I was in high school a couple of decades later, though the only thing we actually knew about her was that she was an old lady with an overbite). And things were even worse in the early years of the Republic. As Ron Chernow observes: "For sheer verbal savagery, the founding era may have surpassed anything seen today."

Chernow is probably right. By historical standards, we don't hear a lot of out-and-out verbal savagery in public life these days, though like every other cultural toxin in the age of the web, it isn't hard to find if you seek it out. What's different about our disputations isn't their intensity or bile so much as their setting and tenor. So if we want to understand the differences between the critics of Lincoln and FDR and the critics of Bush or Obama, evoking "a decline in civility" is not going to be very helpful. The point isn't that we're more or less uncivil, but that we're uncivil in different ways. And in any case, the notion of "incivility" itself is too vague and sententious to be helpful. It doesn't belong to the moral vocabulary of everyday English, like *polite*, *rude*, and *courteous*; it's a word we learn from op-ed pieces, not at the family dinner table. The word is almost impossible to utter innocently: its very mention invites posturing, sermonizing, calls for "national conversations," and simplistic narratives of cultural decay.

The notion of the asshole is a much better place to start. There's a lot to be learned just from tracking the history and use of the word itself. Unlike *civility*, *asshole* operates underneath the radar of reflection. We might deliberate over whether some colleague or relative is better described as an asshole, a prick, or a piece of work, but that's a debate about personalities, not semantics. In fact, people often talk about the word as if it didn't actually have much of a descriptive meaning—even dictionaries are content to define it with vague phrases like "an irritating or contemptible person." In truth, *asshole* is a lot more specific than that, but in any case it isn't a word we acquire from dictionaries or explicit instruction. We learn it through what philosophers call ostensive definition, the same way we learn the meaning of *pink*, *wolf whistle*, and *hook slide,* as in, "There goes one now." Ask people what an asshole is and you're more likely to get a list of names like the one this book opened with than a semantic analysis.

Like the attitude it signals, *asshole* is a very recent addition to our collective life. The insulting use of the word goes back to the GI slang of the 1940s, but it wasn't until 1970 or so that it became a standard category in our moral repertory, a word that could appear in the mouths of characters in Neil Simon plays, Woody Allen movies, and pieces by Tom Wolfe. The modernity of the word reminds us that we're dealing with a new category. Not that being an asshole is a wholly novel kind of social vice. It encompasses a lot of the behavior that was already covered by disapproving epithets like *phony*, *lout*, *heel*, or *cad*. But *asshole* casts our obligations to one another in a different light. And just as important, it implies a right to respond disrespectfully when people disregard those obligations. Actually, you can hardly avoid being disrespectful when you use the word—you can't call somebody an asshole without swearing. That right of response is a principle we've all come to accept in our encounters in parking lots and around the water cooler, however we may like to dilate upon the virtues of forbearance and courtesy in our idealistic moments. Put simply, you have a right to treat assholes as assholes because the assholes have it coming.

I'm going to describe this principle, with no irony intended, as the moral logic of assholism. It brings a delicate social calculus into play. Like stupidity, which it closely resembles, assholism is suffused with moral certainty—not just on the part of the assholes themselves, but also from those who level the charge. Those lists of names people give you to exemplify the word tend to reinforce the idea that assholes are a breed apart, with a distinct and well-defined pathology that makes them different from the rest of us. We tend to think of assholes the way we think about lefties; either you are or you aren't. True, we recognize a distinct temporary state of "being an asshole" or "acting like an asshole," which we sometimes find it useful to cop to by way of manifesting contrition for an uncharacteristic lapse of courtesy or mindfulness (whereas it's rarely a good idea to admit to having been a prick). In that sense *asshole* is very different from a word like *narcissist*. We don't usually say, "God, I was being such a narcissist last night"; with narcissism it's in for a penny, in for a pound. But it would be more realistic and more honest if we talked about a scale of assholism, acknowledging that there are touches of the condition in a lot of the things we do, big and small—one reason why *assholism* is a more useful term than *asshole* is.

This isn't always easy to see, because being an asshole is by nature a form of self-delusion, so that one doesn't recognize it in oneself at the time. I'm always retrospectively mystified by my obtuseness when I look back on some of the things I've done that scream *Asshole!* to me now. But I have no more insight into the conduct than I would if I read about it in a newspaper. And it isn't only at a remove of weeks or years that the veil drops over my past behavior. I can feel that way just a few seconds after I get off the phone with the Comcast customer service representative, as I try to console myself that he must have learned to shrug off customers acting like assholes a long time ago.

Recognizing the deceptive pervasiveness of assholism also involves acknowledging the pleasure that being an asshole can provide, particularly if we have some clear exculpatory provocation in the form of a Comcast overcharge or of someone's stupid political remarks. In our condemnations of assholism, we tend to slide over how gratifying it can be, even vicariously. In fact it can be more pleasurable to watch someone being an asshole to someone you dislike than to be an asshole to them yourself, which after all is rarely free of some suppressed glimmer of guilty self-awareness. The genius of Rush Limbaugh and Stephen Colbert lies in their remarkable ability to convey the pure joy they take in being assholes without suggesting they suffer even the slightest pangs of conscience.

• • •

My main reason for writing this book was to explore the role that the notion of the asshole has come to play in our lives. I don't have a stance on the word, for or against, though I don't see how anyone could condemn it out of hand. There's no end of assholes in the world who deserve to be called out as such. There always have been, though under different titles. At root, the urge to denounce somebody as an asshole is only a modern expression of *saeva indignatio*, the savage indignation that inspired the scabrous satire of Martial and Juvenal, though admittedly the texture of the anger is somewhat different. And anyway, by now the asshole is a stock character in the everyday drama of modern life, even for those of us who don't allow ourselves to pronounce his title. It's a name past repealing.

Still, the asshole as such is also a new addition to the dramatis personae of everyday life, and in the following chapters I'll be tracing the way it has worked its way into the moral lexicon over the past half-century or so. But at this point let me mention just one curious property that makes it different from antecedents like the phony and the heel. It's in the nature of the word *asshole* that it's only appropriate for use in certain contexts. You can't usually print it in a family newspaper, or not nakedly, anyway, even when it's obviously newsworthy. When George W. Bush was overheard on a live mic calling the *New York Times* reporter Adam Clymer an asshole during the 2000 campaign, only a few newspapers were willing to print the word in its orthographic fullness; the others resorted to strategically placed hyphens or asterisks or to coy circumlocutions like "sounds like casserole" or "sounds like glass bowl" (though no one thought to rhyme the word with Picasso the way Jonathan Richman and the Modern Lovers did in a classic 1972 song). The *Washington Times* called it "a vulgar euphemism for a rectal aperture," which suggested a certain confusion about what a euphemism is. The *New York Times* itself, no doubt feeling that asterisks and nudges were beneath the paper's dignity, merely described it as "an obscenity," which made it sound a lot more scabrous than it actually was.★

But why a vulgar name at all? If it were merely a question of charging someone with arrogance or an unwarranted sense of entitlement, we could just as easily have called assholes goobers, say, in which case we could label them for what they are on *Meet the Press* or in a *New York Times* op-ed. By giving this notion a vulgar name, we signal that it can only be appropriately invoked in the settings in which such words are permitted. Of course there are certain publications and certain ranges of the television dial where *asshole* is allowed to appear, but even there, it's almost always put in the mouth of a fictional character or third party rather than used as a direct disparagement, particularly in serious discussion. The word has appeared in the *New Yorker* around 150 times in the last fifteen years or so, and it wouldn't be at all odd to see a story there that quoted the remark Senator Bob Kerry made some years ago about his colleague Rick Santorum: "Santorum—isn't that Latin for asshole?" But a *New Yorker* journalist or

---

★After the story appeared, the *Times*' standards editor, Al Siegel, sent around a memo saying, "Folks: If we have to refer to it again, let's call Bush's word a vulgarity, not an obscenity. It has nothing to do with sex. Nor is it profane, having nothing to do with religion or the deity." That's how I've generally described it here, too. (The *Times* has grown more permissive since then: it reported verbatim the remark George Zimmerman made on the 911 tape just before he shot Trayvon Martin in April 2012: "These assholes, they always get away.")

political writer won't baldly assert, "Rick Santorum is an asshole."★ If the charge can't be leveled in public discussion, it isn't just because the word is vulgar, but because of the values and assumptions it trails.

Or at least that's how things ought to be. What's disquieting about the asshole-baiting style of political discourse is that it tends to efface the line between the conduct appropriate to public and private life. This is a far-reaching modern phenomenon that has a lot of causes: it owes something to the technology of modern communication, something to broad shifts in the cultural background, something to the personalization of political discourse, and something to the deliberate manipulations of the creators of these formats. But the crucial point is that a lot of what people are quick to denounce as the "incivility" of public life isn't necessarily the sign of a moral failing or a collective character disorder, but rather of a muddying of boundaries, a confusion about the proprieties that govern our conduct in different spheres. But before I can return to asking how the moral logic of assholism became an interloper in public life, I want to look at how it works on its native conversational ground.

★The only exception I've found occurred in a 1995 "Talk of the Town" piece by Martin Amis about tennis prima donnas, and even there the charge was coy: Amis described players like McEnroe and Agassi as "personalities," a word he went on to define as "an exact synonym of a seven-letter duosyllable starting with 'a' and ending with 'e' (& also featuring, in order of appearance, an 'ss,' an 'h,' an 'o,' & an 'l')."

chapter two

The Uses of Vulgarity

Frank: Did you say excuse me or something like that?
Learn some manners, asshole.

—**John Bishop,** *The Trip Back Down: A Drama in Two Acts,* **1975**

She turned to look at him. "Before the revolution, asshole,
learn some fucking manners."

—**Nicholas Evans,** *The Divide,* **2007**

The man sitting at the booth slammed his fist into the table
in protest. "You better learn some manners real fast, asshole,"
he warned.

—**Kevin James Sweeney,** *From the Blood of Cain,* **2006**

Rude Words

"Mind your manners, asshole." It ought to be a lame joke, a
blatantly hypocritical utterance like "Watch your mouth,

fuckwad." But it doesn't strike most people as funny right off. In fact it's a cliché that most of us have had occasion to utter, or at least mutter, though sometimes the "mind your manners" part can be dispensed with: a bald "Asshole!" can make the point all by itself.

Indeed, who lives a life so fortunate that the sentence never crosses their mind? *Asshole* is a basic category of our everyday existence, our reflexive remonstrance for people who behave thoughtlessly or arrogantly on the job, in personal relationships, or just circulating in public. It's the word that comes immediately to mind when a neighbor starts his leaf blower at seven-fifteen on Saturday morning or a driver behind us scoots into the parking space we were about to back into. Or if we're being honest with ourselves, it's the word people yell or mutter at us when we do those things, and the one we use to apologize for them on those fleeting occasions when it's given to us to realize how we must have sounded to others. True, there are some of us who won't say the word. The proportion of Americans who claim they never curse runs from 6 to 19 percent, and you figure some of them must be telling the truth. But it's one thing to refuse to let a word pass your lips and another to exclude the concept it stands for from your mental life.

Still, there's a paradoxical irony in appending *asshole* to "mind your manners." *Asshole* is the paradigmatic example of a rude word, in two meanings of *rude*: it's both "indecent, coarse" and "unmannerly, uncivil." So it's striking that it should be the word we instinctively reach for to rebuke inconsiderate behavior. A lot of people would see that as a telling sign of what we've come to: rude even in the way we condemn rudeness. People who deplore the mounting incivility of modern society invariably cite the increase in swearing and foul language as Exhibit A, right up with cell-phone abuse, telemarketers, and aggressive drivers, and a lot of them single out *asshole* for special mention. Pamela Fiori, the editor of *Town and Country*, begins her introduction to a recent anthology of essays from the magazine's Social Graces feature by saying:

> Shortly after I became editor-in-chief of *Town and Country,* I became painfully aware of just how strongly civility was under assault. Forgotten thank-yous and the indiscriminate use of longshoreman's parlance—especially by people who should know better—had become the common currency of social interaction. . . Our behavior toward each other was disintegrating rapidly.

Whether or not they would describe vulgar language with that quaint "longshoreman's parlance," most Americans concur with Fiori's assessment of it baneful effects. In a 2002 Public Agenda survey of attitudes about civility, 84 percent of the respondents said that it bothered them when people use bad or rude language out in public, and three-quarters wanted parents to teach their kids that "cursing is always wrong." Granted, only a few of those people teach that lesson by example. Most of those who disapprove of swearing would concede that they occasionally engage in it themselves, even regrettably *devant les enfants*. But where would swearing be without hypocrisy? To learn what it means to swear, a child has to both hear the words used and be told that it's wrong to use them, ideally by the same people. Every time we tell our children not to use the F-word and then use it ourselves within earshot, we're making a little investment in the future health of profanity.

Still, like some other minor vices, vulgarity is clearly more widely tolerated than it once was. Time was these words were completely absent from polite discourse, and women with pretensions to gentility could go through their life pretending to be ignorant of them. ("She had never heard such words before," a character says in the 1866 novel *Mirk Abbey* of a young lady who has witnessed an altercation, "and could scarcely force her innocent lips to repeat them.") In our age, vulgarity, like slot machines and beachside nudity, is permitted in designated areas and prohibited in others. Words that were okay in *Sex and the City* when it ran on pay cable had to be bleeped on free cable and replaced by anodyne equivalents when the show was run on broadcast television. So if many people still disapprove of vulgarity in principle, it's hard to find anyone who can honestly claim to be scandalized by it. Nowadays, in fact, critics of vulgarity are often at pains to demonstrate their worldliness, and the words are much more likely to be criticized as uncivil than as indecent. When people praised a figure like the legendary UCLA basketball coach John Wooden for never swearing, it was meant as a testimony to his even-temperedness, not his purity of mind.

Nowadays, in fact, the objection to vulgarity is often made on purely stylistic grounds. The problem with dirty words like *asshole* isn't so much that they're dirty, critics say, as that they're a sign of mental laziness or a defective vocabulary. That's what's implied when we speak of someone "resorting to" vulgarity, as if it were the recourse of those who can't be bothered to come up with a more apt and expressive term. Melissa Caldwell, the director of research for the Parents Television Council watchdog group, says that profanity doesn't just lead to violent acts but impoverishes the English language. In *Cuss Control: The Complete Book on How to Curb Your Cursing*, James V. O'Connor condemns *asshole* as vague and urges readers to eschew it for more amusing or unexpected terms, such as *cad*, *cur*, *heel*, or *rogue*—or better still, to come up with a "clever and imaginative put-down" that will "help you blow off steam while adding luster to your reputation as an astute wit." And while the Yale legal scholar Stephen Carter doesn't explicitly mention *asshole* in his 1998 book *Civility: Manners, Morals, and the Etiquette of Democracy*, the word clearly wasn't far from his mind when he deplored the substitution of vulgar epithets for the eloquent contumely of the past:

> The nineteenth and early twentieth centuries offered a tradition of public insults that were witty, pointed, occasionally cruel, but not obscene or particularly offensive. Nowadays the tradition of barbed wit has given way to a witless barbarism . . . we prefer, animal-like, to make the first sound that comes to mind.

Those passages sum up the prevailing wisdom about vulgar words in general and *asshole* in particular: they're rude, abusive, lazy, vague, artless, and impulsive—not really words at all but animal noises, the first sounds that come to mind.

The Necessary Delusions of Vulgarity

None of that is even remotely true, but if we didn't believe it the words couldn't accomplish their useful work. The basic point of swearing, after all, is to demonstrate that your emotions have gotten the better of you. As Erving Goffman put it, swearing is "a form of behavior whose very meaning is that it is something blurted out, something that has escaped control." In that way swear words are similar to words such as *ouch!, ick!,* and *whee!* that linguists call expressives. They don't describe sensations but manifest them: crying "ouch!" is not the same thing as saying "I am in pain at this moment." It seems natural to think of vulgar words in the same way—they serve to vent or to abuse, rather than to describe. Once a word becomes an insult, Robert Musil wrote, it no longer stands for what it signifies, "but for a mixture of ideas, feelings, and intentions which it can not even remotely express, but which it can signal."

But these are, as I say, just useful misconceptions. For one thing, vulgarities aren't the impulsive ejaculations that people make them out to be. Swearing isn't like sneezing: we aren't powerless to control our tongues, however strong the emotions of the moment. As Goffman remarked, "A man who utters *fuck* when he stumbles in a foundry is quite likely to avoid that particular expletive should he trip in a day nursery." Indeed, an inability to exert such self-control is regarded as a symptom of a neurological disorder.

Nor are the words meaningless or even especially vague. It's a common preconception that slang words are vaguer but more vivid than formal vocabulary—that they denote less, and connote more, than other words do. As it happens, the highfalutin' word is often vaguer than its colloquial cousin: most people are a lot clearer on *raunchy* than on *prurient*. But when a slang word is vulgar in the bargain, there's a strong temptation to assume that its function as an insult pretty much exhausts its meaning. It's an assumption shared even by lexicographers, who of all people ought to be attentive to nuances of meaning. The *Oxford English Dictionary* (*OED*) defines *asshole* simply as "someone foolish or contemptible; an uncompromising term of abuse." That's roughly the same as the definitions the dictionary gives for *shit* ("a contemptuous epithet applied to a person"), *prick* ("a vulgar term of abuse for a man"), *fuckwad* ("a foolish or contemptible person; also as a term of abuse"), and *cocksucker* ("used as a generalized term of abuse"). A foreigner who consulted the *OED* for elucidation of the fine points of English malediction could be excused for concluding that the words are freely interchangeable.

Now there are some words that seem to function almost entirely as empty terms of abuse. When you call someone a motherfucker, about the only thing you convey is that you don't much care for him. The word is mostly used either as a direct insult, as in "You motherfucker!" or as a kind of pronoun of contempt, as in "Clancy was supposed to get the tickets, but I haven't heard from the motherfucker." But *asshole* has a quite specific meaning that distinguishes it from *shit*, *prick,* and the others. When we call somebody an asshole, it's because we've decided that that's the shoe that fits him best. You wouldn't say that the meaning of the word is precise, but then the words that express social evaluations almost never are. When you come down to it, *asshole* is no vaguer than *boor* or *scoundrel*, or for that matter than the notoriously elusive word *gentleman*.

Yet there's a fair consensus about what kinds of behavior qualify someone for the asshole label, and they're only a fraction of the things you could do to make yourself "foolish or contemptible," as the *OED* defines the word. You can be an asshole for abruptly cutting into a line of cars waiting in the left-turn lane, but probably not for failing to signal a turn or texting while you drive. You can be an asshole for cheating on your wife or girlfriend, but not for cheating on your expense reports or a final exam. You can be an asshole for taking credit for a colleague's work, but probably not for plagiarizing from someone else's book. A CEO may count as an asshole if he yells at his assistants or makes sexual advances to women employees, but not if he simply gets his board to pay him a bloated compensation package. And even if you believe that George W. Bush lied about WMDs in Iraq, that by itself wouldn't make him an asshole, though he might have earned the label for his press-conference smirks. Of course you can cook up scenarios in which any one of these things might qualify someone an asshole, but it takes some additional background. If I simply say that I caught a student cheating on his final, you wouldn't be likely to remark, "What an asshole!" unless we both knew that there was more to the story than that.

No other word carves out the same exact range of misconduct that *asshole* does. Not all people who are assholes are arrogant, pretentious, or unmannerly, and vice versa. And there's invariably a loss of precision or color when we forbear from calling someone an asshole in favor of one of the more respectable labels that critics recommend, like *boor, lout,* or *bully. Jerk* comes closest. It's the word usually chosen by people who want to convey the meaning of *asshole* without actually using the word, like the writer of *Cosmopolitan*'s online advice column:

> That guy you went out with is a freakin' jerk, and you're much better off without him. It's one thing to expect sex; it's quite another to act like an irate ass when you don't get it.

"Freakin' jerk" here is clearly just a sanitized version of *fucking asshole.* And lest there be any doubt about the point, the writer adds a reference to *ass,* an insult which Americans now derive from the word for derrières rather than for donkeys, and whose metaphorical meaning has shifted from silliness to arrogance due to its semantic and anatomical proximity to *asshole.* (The shift in literal meaning has made the insult *ass* sound a lot more vulgar than it once did; students are taken aback when they see Henry James or T. S. Eliot describing someone with the word.)

But even when it's used as a proxy for *asshole, jerk* can't connote the same brazen effrontery (on the web, *asshole* is fifty times more likely than *jerk* to be modified by "screaming" or "flaming"). In fact *jerk* can sometimes be a term of endearment. "I'm in love with you, you jerk!" Jennifer Love Hewitt tells Scott Wolf in *Party of Five,* a line that would sound a lot less darling if *asshole* were used instead. (Or recall Howard Hawks' 1941 *Ball of Fire,* when Barbara Stanwyck says about Gary Cooper's character, "I love him because he doesn't know how to kiss, the jerk!" Even if *asshole* had been around back then, you can be sure that nobody would have used it of any character played by Gary Cooper.) Similarly for the retro or "amusing" substitutes for *asshole* that O'Connor suggests, which usually strike us as denatured euphemisms for the A-word, even in extraterrestrial settings:

> HAN SOLO: Come on, admit it. Sometimes you think I'm all right.
>
> PRINCESS LEIA: Occasionally maybe . . . when you aren't acting like a scoundrel.
>
> HAN SOLO: Scoundrel? Scoundrel? I like the sound of that.

Adult viewers understand that *scoundrel* here is simply the word you use when you're translating the dialog from *When Harry Met Sally* for rebroadcast a long time ago in a galaxy far away. After all, this is an exchange between Carrie Fisher and Harrison Ford, not Olivia de Havilland and Errol Flynn.

How to Do Things with Bad Words

Ultimately, what makes *asshole* distinctive is the way it's used, the speech-acts it allows us to perform. These begin, obviously, with the meaning of the word, the traits that define the particular offenders it singles out. Ask people to characterize an asshole, and they'll mention arrogance, pretension, egotism, rudeness, or an overblown sense of entitlement. But those don't pin the word down by themselves; they're like a list of symptoms that manifest the underlying disorder. At the heart of assholism is a culpable obtuseness—about one's own importance, about the needs of others and the way one is perceived by them. Being an asshole always involves a particular form of stupidity (on the web, *asshole* is six times as likely as *prick* to be modified by *dumb*). By purely ethical standards, being an asshole is probably less blameworthy than being a shit or a heel, since the latter have no delusions about how they're seen or what they're doing: unlike the asshole, they have an accurate moral compass but choose to disregard it. And indeed the asshole is better suited to play a comic villain than a truly evil character: you think of Malvolio in *Twelfth Night*, not Iago in *Othello*; of the martinet assistant principal or despotic football coach in a high-school comedy, not Dennis Hopper in *Blue Velvet*. Yet for most of us, it stings more to be thought of as an asshole than as a heel or a bastard, for the same reason that in the schoolyard, "you're stupid" cuts more deeply than "you're mean." To be a heel or a shit is at least to be recognized and detested—*Oderint dum metuant*, as Caligula liked to say, "Let them hate so long as they fear." Whereas *asshole* cuts the ground out from under us, denying our self-perceptions and our pretensions to worth: it tells us that we don't even see how inconsequential and contemptible we are.

That, at least, is the dictionary meaning of *asshole* (or would be, if lexicographers didn't have a blind spot about the meanings of obscenities). But an account of the significance of a word doesn't stop at its denotative meaning: there's also its force. By that I mean not simply the approval or disapproval it expresses, but its power to evoke emotions that the meaning alone doesn't explain. Think of derogative words. *Promiscuity* covers a lot of the same ground that *sluttiness* does, but it isn't colored with the same derision. Similarly, saying that *asshole* imputes arrogance or pretension to someone doesn't explain the contempt it conveys.

The metaphor obviously has a lot to do with that. Likening someone to the anus suggests that he is small, foul, noisome, and low, as we conventionally view that anatomical feature. (There can be dissenting views, of course. "The asshole is holy," Allen Ginsberg famously wrote in "Howl," but he was trying to make a point.) It seems an appropriate comparison for someone who thinks himself more important or grander than he has a right to, and it's not surprising that there are variants of the same theme in the vulgar words meaning "turd" or "pubic hair" that roughly translate *asshole* in other languages. But if the force of the word were just a matter of the vividness of the image it suggests, there are other sorts of metaphors that could have the same effect. The woods are literally full of malignant things that lend themselves to the creation of terms of insult: skunks, rats, swine, weasels, maggots, snakes, toads, worms, and all the other beasties that English-speakers have conscripted for their insults since Chaucer's time, whose names, unlike *asshole*, have the advantage of being printable in a family newspaper.

But unlike *worm* or *maggot*, *asshole* is a dirty word, which is to say that whenever we use it we're flouting the norms of propriety, even in settings where flouting such norms is routine and swearing is virtually compulsory. You can't pronounce *asshole* without evoking the people who disapprove of it—the shades of absent parents, teachers, supervisors, officers, or simply an archetypal prude—and placing yourself, at least symbolically, outside the circle of polite conversation.

The vulgarity of *asshole* makes a big difference: it limits the contexts where the word can be used and magnifies its force, and it can create a special bond with the listener.

We think of *asshole* as typically a face-to-face insult—the use that dictionaries are describing when they define the word as a "term of abuse," and the one I had in mind when I began this chapter by talking about "Mind your manners, asshole." In that situation, saying "asshole!" can be a way of demonstrating that your emotions have overcome your inhibitions, as Goffman suggested. Or it can be a pointed show of disdain, as if your addressee isn't worthy of the respect that observance of the norms of polite conversation ordinarily conveys. One way or the other, when you call someone an asshole to his face you're not simply describing him. You're making a literal display of anger and contempt, like a rhesus monkey baring his teeth and pounding the ground with his palms. Whether the feelings are genuine or assumed, what matters is your willingness to make the gesture. It's an act of symbolic violence, and in that sense *asshole* doesn't simply arraign someone for his misconduct as *jerk* or *maggot* do. It's also a retribution—or when we turn it on ourselves, a kind of self-flagellation.

But in actual practice we less often use *asshole* as a direct insult than to refer to some third party who's out of earshot. In those cases the word's vulgarity serves not just to make a display of our indignation but also to create a sense of complicity or solidarity with the listener. *Asshole* was first converted to a personal description in the barracks slang of World War II, and ever since then it has been a label for an arrogant or overbearing superior—a way of bringing someone down to our level and denying him the respect or deference he seems to feel he deserves. Among co-workers, it joins us in a shared defiance of absent authorities, with a hint of the furtive pleasure we took in schoolyard swearing as potty-mouthed children. Among friends and family, it takes down the pretension or presumption of in-laws, neighbors, and schoolmates.

Or in a variant of that, we may call somebody an asshole in order to commiserate with the people he has offended or injured. There are times when *asshole* isn't simply the *mot juste* but the *mot de rigueur*. A friend calls to tell you she has just discovered that her husband has been having an affair with the nanny. You're not about to respond by saying, "*Sacre bleu!* How caddish!" or by improvising some novel malediction that invites admiration for your cleverness—this isn't about you, after all. Common decency requires that you simply say, "What an asshole!" thereby not just condemning the offense and manifesting your contempt for the offender, but also inviting your listener to replace her feelings of hurt and diminution with a restorative anger.

In one way or another, *asshole* indicates a failure to show the respect we owe one another in virtue of our common humanity, independent of any disparities in power or status. *Asshole* levels us, but always downwards: it creates an impression of proletarian solidarity even long after we've put schoolyards, barracks, and cubicle farms behind us. That's one place where the word can get tricky. If it's the natural response of a subordinate to a superior, it can carry an undertone of arrogance when it's directed the other way, as a way of closing ranks against an upstart. That businessman who's indignantly berating the airport gate agent for not giving him an upgrade as we wait to board the plane makes it almost automatic to mutter, "What an asshole!" to the person standing next to us—always provided that we're in the line for economy boarding. Coming from someone in the first-class line, there's a chance that sentence will sound like the smug contempt for a parvenu. To use *asshole* is usually to evoke the shadow of class, even if it's only of the variety you can attain for a few thousand mileage points.

De Haut en Bush

The specter of class colored the utterance by George W. Bush that was caught on mic at an appearance in Naperville, Illinois, during the 2000 presidential campaign. Turning to Dick Cheney, Bush said, "There's Adam Clymer, major league asshole from the *New York Times*," to which Cheney responded, "Oh, yeah, he is. Big time." The incident provoked a blizzard of commentary, which illustrated most of the varieties of humbug and hypocrisy that vulgarity invariably evokes when it bubbles into public view. To Bush's critics, the remark discredited his pledge to restore civility to politics. As the *Boston Globe*'s David Nyhan put it: "So much for the Civility Boyz. The pair that vowed piously to bring civility back into national politics took a Labor Day header into a dry swimming pool." Dan Rather charged the candidate with using "gutter language," and *Newsweek* spoke of the "bar-talk crudeness" that would undermine his image as "a genial, upbeat outsider determined to restore civility to the rude business of politics." And a Gore spokesman described Bush as "using expletives to describe a *New York Times* reporter in front of a crowd of families," which was literally correct but utterly misleading.

Meanwhile, Bush's defenders were making the predictable comparisons to Harry Truman and claiming that the incident demonstrated their candidate's plain-spoken moxie. In the *New York Post*, Steve Dunleavy said that the remark showed that Bush was still a "knockabout Texas fly-boy," and urged him not to apologize for it—rather he should look Clymer straight in the eye and tell him he meant every word he said: "Everyone, from workers in factories in Gary, Ind., to farmers in Nebraska, will stand and applaud." And the columnist Cal Thomas, comparing Bush to the "scripted" Al Gore, urged Bush to "Tell it like it is. . . . if some reporters resemble what a proctologist sees in the office, the public will thank you for pointing that out."

This was all pure sham, on both sides. "Bar-talk crudeness," "gutter language"—was the A-word really alien to the inner sanctums of CBS or *Newsweek*? (Shocked, shocked, to find that swearing is going on!) The fact is that there was nothing uncivil about the remark. After all, Bush hadn't called Clymer an asshole to his face, much less in a public forum, so he had no need to apologize, beyond saying he regretted other people had heard it. On the other hand, Bush's private aside to Cheney wasn't anything like the hell's and damn's with which Truman peppered his speeches; if you were looking for a historical parallel, the remark was less Trumanesque than Nixonian. And merely using the word *asshole* hardly establishes that you're a true man of the people, or for that matter, a true man. It's doubtful whether those Nebraska farmers or Indiana factory workers would have taken it as evidence that Bush was

One of Us—for one thing, they don't modify *asshole* with *major league* or *big-time*, expressions you associate with superannuated Yalies, not steelworkers.

In fact both critics and defenders were appealing to the same proletarian caricature associated with vulgar language. That's another of the delusions that are essential to enabling these words to do their work; we still speak of someone swearing like a truck driver or longshoreman even though the words have been thoroughly integrated into middle-class English for several generations. According to the situation, the proles in question can be regarded as gutter lowlifes or honest, plain-spoken yeomen, but there's no partisan cast to that choice. When a Democrat is caught out using a blue word, other Democrats generally give him a pass. "Yes, Mr. Vice President, you're right," the White House press secretary Robert Gibbs tweeted after Joe Biden was caught on mic at the signing of the 2010 health care bill whispering to the president, "This is a big fucking deal." Republicans, not surprisingly, were dismayed and indignant. "I'm very disappointed that he would use that kind of language," Bush's press secretary Andrew Card said when John Kerry said that Bush had fucked up the Iraq war.

Those reactions are automatic no matter which vulgar word happens to be used. But Bush's choice of *asshole* in particular enabled his defenders to applaud him for corroborating what they had been saying about the media's inflated sense of self-importance, as if being an asshole wasn't a personal defect of Clymer so much as a *déformation professionnelle*. As William Powers put the charge in *National Journal*, "The journalistic establishment is like one big, pretentious snot-nosed French waiter." And Jonah Goldberg took the occasion to observe that "most people see the press as an arrogant and unaccountable priesthood of kingmakers or, in the common vernacular, @$#&*!s." It was a perfect example of the assholization of political differences—if the media's coverage is animated by pretension and arrogance, then you can dismiss it out of hand. In normal circumstances, of course, the right's media critics wouldn't have made their point by appealing to the A-word. But since Bush brought it up. . . .

In truth, there was nothing in the remark to suggest that Bush was offering a general comment on the media. It wasn't impersonal: he and Cheney obviously felt that Clymer had it in for them and was tilting his reporting accordingly. But even if that was right, the remark was still awkward. A powerful political figure can't describe his media critics as assholes without sounding like he's taxing them for being uppity. Unfairly or not, the exchange brought to mind a couple of fraternity jocks maligning the freshman nerd who had turned them in for cheating on an exam. Calling somebody an asshole can sometimes be an assholish thing to do.

Having a Word for It

The Bush contretemps demonstrated just how broad a range of attitudes *asshole* brings into play—about civil behavior, about emotion and expression, about authenticity, about gender, about class and power, and about sex and the body. Historically, the concept of the asshole emerged out of the interaction of those attitudes, and the word *asshole* was coined to express it. People had to see the world as populated with assholes before they could come up with a name for them. But there's also a sense in which the word gave form to the concept and made it tangible to the community. If we didn't have a name for assholes they couldn't figure as categories in our collective moral life.

Does our language shape our ideas or do our ideas shape our language? The answer to both questions is yes. The common view is that having a word for something is a precondition for having the concept: if you can't put a name on it, you can't really think of it. As Lionel Trilling said, lamenting the disappearance of the use of *disinterested* to mean having no stake in an outcome, "I fear this is a lost cause. I take it very hard—without the word we can't have the thing." In one form or another, that picture recurs in most of the stories we tell about language. It's embodied in Orwell's fable of Newspeak, a language whose vocabulary has been pared down to the point where it makes seditious thoughts impossible: "It would have been possible to say 'Big Brother is ungood.' But this statement . . . could not have been sustained by reasoned argument, because the necessary words were not available." It's evoked by the linguistic chauvinists who say that immigrants ignorant of English can't conceptualize the tenets of democracy that are built into our vocabulary—what one writer calls "the inherent capability of the English language to define and exhort the essence and spirit of government by consent of the governed." And it's implicit in the observations people are always offering about the lexical deficiencies of this or that language: French doesn't have a word for "nice," German doesn't have a word for "fair play," Arabic doesn't have a word for "compromise," Chinese doesn't have a word for "privacy," and so on, always with the implication that those cultures must therefore lack the corresponding idea.

As it happens, those stories about lexical gaps are usually incorrect or misleading. A language that lacks a single word for "compromise" can accomplish exactly the same purpose with a phrase like "come to terms" or "meet each other halfway" (the concept of bargaining isn't exactly alien to the cultures of the Middle East, after all). But even when the claims happen to be true, it doesn't follow that the concept is either unthinkable or inexpressible—if it's important to people, they'll find a way to get it across. We don't have either a word or common phrase that translates the German *Schadenfreude*, the pleasure one takes in the misfortunes of others. But that doesn't mean that Red Sox fans have to learn German before they can enjoy watching the Yankees lose the World Series in four straight games. In fact a people can have a concept at its disposal for a very long time before they feel the need to give it a specific name. English didn't have the word *patriotism* until the mid–eighteenth century. But to anyone who recalls John of Gaunt's speech from Richard II ("This throne of kings, this scepter'd isle . . . the other Eden, demi-paradise"), it's clear not just that the Elizabethans loved their country, but that they understood the idea of loving one's country.

Take these observations to their logical conclusion, and you come to an opposing view, which is popular among linguists and philosophers: language doesn't play much of a role in determining thought and doesn't impose any limit on the ideas you can formulate. True, there are advantages to having a word for such-and-such a concept, but only because it's a convenient form of packaging. Coining *carbon-neutral* saved us the trouble of having to say "relating to the maintenance of a balance between producing and using carbon, especially balancing carbon dioxide emissions by activities such as growing plants to use as fuel or planting trees in urban areas to offset vehicle emissions," as the *Encarta Dictionary* pithily defines it. The phrase has certainly made it easier to store the notion mentally and communicate it to others. As this view is explained by Steven Pinker, who's one of its best-known advocates:

> If a language provides a label for a complex concept, that could make it easier to think about the concept, because the mind can handle it as a single package when juggling a set of ideas, rather than having to keep each of its components in the air separately.

But all we can conclude from this is that "the stock of words in language reflects the kinds of things its speakers deal with in their lives and hence think about." Seen that way, the appearance of a new word can only testify either to a heightened interest in an old topic or the introduction of a new one, often as a result of some technological innovation or social trend. That's how we think of words like *app, tweet, metrosexual, locovore,* and *tiger mom.* Those are the material signs of cultural change which journalists like to track and which tend to figure as finalists in the word-of-the-year lists compiled by dictionaries and dialect scholars. But while words like these are often clever, they can only herald the appearance of a new phenomenon, rather than shaping or creating one. We didn't need the evidence of *unfriend* to learn that social networking had become a major phenomenon.

But sometimes we introduce a new word not to name a new concept but to color a familiar one with a particular point of view. The eighteenth-century appearance of *patriotism* didn't signify that the British had suddenly discovered the love of country but rather that the claim to love one's country had become controversial, a part of "the hard currency of party rhetoric," as the historian Mary G. Dietz put it, which is what led Dr. Johnson to denounce it as "the last refuge of a scoundrel." The label was needed not to name the phenomenon but to enable people to express a particular attitude about it—though with time, that attitude shifted from scorn to uncritical approval. We didn't need *patriotism*, that is, until the love of one's country became a topic that people took a position on. That's why we don't need a word for the love of one's mother—it's not a position we're ever going to be called on to defend.

Think of this as the Caliban principle: sometimes we give things names so that we can curse them. There have always been young, upwardly mobile professionals. But before the introduction of *yuppie* they didn't have a fixed place in the social bestiary: you could assert that such people were superficial and materialist, but you couldn't refer to them in a way that simply presumed that. In fact *yuppie* was only one of a number of terms that emerged between the late 1960s and early 1980s to redefine social class in terms of the categories of consumer culture: new words like *upscale* and *trendy* and newly redefined ones like *lifestyle*, *preppie*, and *demographics*. The words could only follow on the emergence of the attitudes they conveyed. But they confirmed the attitudes as cultural reference points—the very fact of their wide acceptance meant that you didn't have to explain or justify the point they made ("Yuppies—need I say more?").

It's those attitudes as much as their referential meanings that can make words "untranslatable," not just across languages but also from one era to the next. It's easy to find literary and historical antecedents for modern yuppies; the Victorian age was full of young middle-class people on the make. But we can't label them with that word except by way of making an arch little joke with the reader. John Bayley once described Trollope as "the yuppie beau ideal," but the attitude the word itself expresses isn't one that Trollope himself could have entertained, no more than he could have made sense of *Bright Lights, Big City* or a Sharper Image catalogue.

In that way, new words don't simply reflect changes in ideas and attitudes, they crystallize them. And the more abstract and amorphous the changes are—the less they're tied to material things, the more they're concerned purely with values or sensibilities—the harder it is to identify and pin them without reference to the words that embody them. Take *cool*. Since it first entered the linguistic mainstream in the 1950s, it has managed to survive the retrenchment of one after another of the groups and trends it was associated with (the hipster, the hippie, the surfer, the digerato, and now the hipster redux) as it threw off new idioms and derivatives in each iteration: *cool cat*, *uncool*, *way cool*, *coolio*. It isn't easy to say what it means— it's no doubt uncool to try. But we know it when we see it, and through all its transformations, it seems to be an abiding modern sensibility. And once you grasp the idea of cool, you can examine it as modern cultural phenomenon, as the historian Peter N. Stearns has in *American Cool: Constructing a Twentieth-Century Emotional Style*. Stearns demonstrates convincingly that the style we call cool began to take form long before the word itself entered the mainstream vocabulary. But would we perceive that line of sensibility if there had never been a word to express it—if *cool* had never appeared, or if it had vanished around 1960 with the rest of hipster slang, like *reet* and *solid*?

The Assholization of the Moral Life

"Now and then," Lionel Trilling wrote at the beginning of *Sincerity and Authenticity,* "it is possible to observe the moral life in process of revising itself." Trilling was speaking of the rise of the notion of sincerity in the modern era, when being "true to oneself" was added to the inventory of social virtues. But one could say the same of the cultural upheavals that accompanied the rise of *asshole* in the sixties and seventies, in what we still think of as a transitional moment a half century later. Things once unthinkable were becoming acceptable and even commendable; things once unexceptionable were becoming objectionable or even obnoxious. Watching the reconstruction of upper-middle-class American life during the early 1960s in the TV show *Mad Men*, you're taken back to an age when no one saw anything offensive in telling racist and anti-Semitic jokes or lighting a cigarette at the table while others were still eating, and when value-charged notions like "diversity," "sexism," "homophobia," "green," and "date rape" would have been almost as difficult to get across as the notion of sincerity would have been in the age of Homer. The past is a foreign country: they smoke at the dinner table.

The additions to our moral vocabularies don't always involve creating a new virtue or vice out of whole cloth, the way *sincerity* did in the seventeenth century or that *homophobia* or *date rape* do now. Often it's a matter of refashioning the ones that are already on the table. When the banker Mr. Merdle in *Little Dorrit* is revealed to be a swindler who has destituted all those who trusted in him, Dickens describes him as a "mighty scoundrel":

> Numbers of men in every profession and trade would be blighted by his insolvency; old people who had been in easy circumstances all their lives would have no place of repentance for their trust in him but the workhouse; legions of women and children would have their whole future desolated by the hand of this mighty scoundrel.

When Bernard Madoff does exactly the same thing now, he's reviled as a sociopath or a scumbag. But it isn't as if Madoff's crime is considered either more or less heinous than Merdle's was; it's just that we have different notions about the source of Madoff's moral failing and of the trust that he violated. Similarly, the Victorians' *humbug* and *gammon* evolved into *bunk* and *bilge* and then into *bullshit*, but we haven't vacillated in our basic contempt for pretension and obfuscatory nonsense.

Asshole is similar. From one point of view, being an asshole isn't really a newly discovered vice like homophobia or date rape. The characters we've been talking about—the passenger irately demanding an upgrade at the gate, the husband who runs off with the au pair—would have been contemptible in earlier ages, whatever label they were given. That's why it's so easy to naturalize the asshole, as if assholes had been an eternal and universal plague of human societies from the time when Achilles sat sulking in his tent while the war was going badly for his fellow Greeks. So what if the asshole didn't actually make his first appearance under that very name until the middle of the twentieth century? There certainly seem to be enough examples of the type in the novels of Trollope, Thackeray, and Austen. Think of the smarmy clergyman Mr. Collins in *Pride and Prejudice*—what better model could there be for the self-important, name-dropping assholes that modern life is swollen with?

> . . . most fortunately having it in our power to introduce you
> to very superior society, and from our connection with Ros-
> ings, the frequent means of varying the humble home scene,
> I think we may flatter ourselves that your Hunsford visit can-
> not have been entirely irksome.

And don't forget Darcy, either, initially disparaging Elizabeth Bennet's looks ("not handsome enough to tempt *me*") and later, following his declaration of love by asking her to appreciate his misgivings about allying himself with someone of her modest station:

> Could you expect me to rejoice in the inferiority of your con-
> nections?—to congratulate myself on the hope of relations,
> whose condition in life is so decidedly beneath my own?

What modern reader can come on that passage without mut-
tering, "Sheesh, what an asshole"?—though to be sure of a
different phylum from Mr. Collins, one capable of repenting
his haughtiness and turning into Colin Firth.

But calling Collins or Darcy an asshole isn't simply a linguistic anachronism, like calling Pemberley a dope crib.
Austen and her contemporary readers wouldn't really have
understood the concept of the asshole at all, even under a
more anodyne name. They disapproved of Darcy's conduct,
but not because he had reservations about marrying beneath
his class; they would have found that "natural and just," exactly
as he did. His real offense lay in his vain self-congratulation
for having overcome those scruples and his ungentlemanlike
cluelessness in imagining that Elizabeth would find that to his
credit. That's typical of the differences in understanding that
are implicit in the labels other periods gave to the characters
who strike us now as assholes—*popinjay, whelp, chuff, coxcomb,
bounder, cad, ass,* or *heel,* to name a few. They come down on
the offenses with equal severity, but they characterize them
differently, the way new medical diagnoses reclassify familiar
conditions according to a new understanding of their etiolo-
gies.

But *asshole* involves two kinds of innovations. The word itself introduced a new category that remapped the territory
once marked off by *heel, cad,* and the others. But *asshole*

doesn't just identify a type of person that never had a single name before; it also does so, oddly, by means of a vulgar name. I say "oddly" because really there's no logical reason for why the word we use to refer to these people should have an obscene origin. There's nothing inherently indecent or obscene in the category itself. When you attach the word *asshole* to some public figure whom you consider egregiously obnoxious you might be taking him to task for arrogance, thoughtlessness, or conceit, but you're not implying anything about his sexual predilections or bodily hygiene. Indeed, you're not making any allegation that you couldn't repeat on Sunday morning network television, provided you reframed it in more decorous language.

As a name for a certain type of person, *asshole* comes by its taint second hand, as what the legal scholar Joel Feinberg calls a "derivative obscenity." When it's used literally, an obscene word acquires its stigma from the thing it names. ("A nasty name for a nasty thing," as Captain Grose's 1788 *Dictionary of the Vulgar Tongue* says in its entry under *c**t*, as it rendered the word.) But when the word is used figuratively, the stigma is passed on via a kind of contagious magic, to pick up the term Sir James Fraser used in *The Golden Bough*. Once a word is polluted, it retains its taboo when it is reassigned a new, aseptic reference, or even when it's buried inside another word. As primitive or exotic as the principle may sound, it's familiar to every child—think of the illicit pleasure that a four-year-old takes in pronouncing *shamPOO*. As grown-ups, of course, we disabuse ourselves of the idea that the syllables of such words really have magical powers, but we still react to them as if they did. That's why the force of the words can't be con-

tained in quotation marks and the other devices that we ordinarily use to keep the meaning of a word at arm's length
(semantically, they work as a kind of universal solvent). Yet the
words can be decontaminated by the simple expedient of replacing their vowels with asterisks or bleeping a syllable. A
magical spell has no power unless you say it just so.

But while the process of creating secondhand vulgarities has
always been available to speakers of English, they rarely made
use of it before modern times. There have always been taboo
words for body parts, sex, and elimination, of course, and
they've sometimes been applied to people, usually with a scatological or erotic overtone. In the Renaissance, *turd* was a term
of execration and *prick* could be a lewd endearment for a
young man (the *OED* exemplifies it with a line from a seven-
teenth-century text: "Ah, ha! Are we not alone, my prick? Let
us go together into my inner bed-chamber"). But it wasn't
until about a century ago that English began to create the pro-
fusion of dirty words for clean things that gives our conversation its modern stamp, from *bullshit* to *pissed off* to *shitty* to a
clutch of idiomatic phrases beginning with *fuck* (-*around*,-*off*,
up,-*over*,-*all*). These were new words, as surely as *mouse* is a
new word when it refers to a computer pointing device.

It's really vocabularies, rather than individual words, that
are the units of lexical change—groups of words that share a
common form or origin and that are connected by some
common theme. *Patriotism* was one of a clutch of political
isms that entered the language in the eighteenth century, including *fanaticism, republicanism, despotism,* and *ism* itself, most
of them with a disparaging cast—Metternich said that all isms
were abusive. *Yuppie* came in with a number of shorter-lived

items from marketing jargon like *buppie, bobo,* and DINK ("double income no kids"). Or take the successive waves of French borrowings that English has absorbed in modern times, most of them reflecting Gallic stereotypes—words that suggest cosmopolitan sophistication, like *debonair, chic,* and *à la mode,* or that permit us to talk about naughty things with a more urbane tolerance than our Anglo-Saxon attitudes ordinarily countenance, like *affair, risqué,* and *ménage à trois.*

Asshole and its vulgar fellows have something in common with those French words. They entered the standard language as borrowings, as well, though they came up from the ranks rather than trickling down from a Francophile elite. And like the French loans for naughty things, they suggest notions that it would be inappropriate to have words for in the language that expresses our acknowledged public values. But the motivations for coining the new vulgarisms are a bit less obvious. There's no mystery about people's reasons for importing words from French—delicacy, pretension, or the deference to French preeminence in the domestic arts that gave us *décor, lingerie,* and *chef.* But why did twentieth-century English-speakers feel the need to create a new vocabulary derived from obscene words?

The reflexive answer is to point to the repudiation of Victorian taboos about talking about sex and the body, whether one goes on to describe that as a liberation or a coarsening of the culture. And it's true there's some connection here. When you loosen the inhibitions about pronouncing the syllable *fuck* in its literal meaning, you also make it more acceptable to use the word as an expression of exasperation or to combine it with *off* to form a phrase for loaf or shirk (though in general we tend to be more circumspect about the former—a lot of people who have no qualms about saying, "They're fucking crazy" would have more compunctions about saying, "They're fucking"). But as we'll see, the literal and figurative uses of these words had very different motivations and social origins: D. H. Lawrence and David Mamet aren't drawing from the same linguistic well. Indeed the literal and figurative uses tend to work at cross-purposes: the disinhibition that encourages the first tends to weaken the second. If there's still some shock value to calling somebody a fucking prick, it's because we haven't wholly abandoned our conviction that there's still something shameful about sex and the body. And however our attitudes about those things have changed, none of this explains why we should have transformed the obscene names for them into new words that had nothing to do with either.

The redeployment of these words was only incidentally connected to new attitudes about sex—it had more to do with attitudes about class, emotion, self-expression, and the moral grounding of everyday life. And it's here that we need to look to find the connection between the vulgarity of these words and their meanings. The connection isn't obvious, as I said—or at least not as obvious as the reasons for importing *chic* or *démodé*. There's a temptation to think of vulgarity as simply an ancillary feature of the words, which is the picture that dictionaries imply with the usage labels they tack on to their entries:

asshole (*American Heritage*): 2. *Vulgar Slang* A thoroughly contemptible, detestable person.

bullshit (*Merriam-Webster*): *usually vulgar* nonsense;
especially: foolish insolent talk

The idea behind these labels is that the difference between a vulgar word and a respectable one is basically a matter of where and when you can say them, rather than of their meanings, like the difference between the colloquial word *guy* and the neutral word *man*. That's the assumption that Harry G. Frankfurt made in *On Bullshit*. At one point Frankfurt compares *bullshit* to *humbug*, and concludes that while the two aren't freely interchangeable, that's mostly a matter of "considerations of gentility": while *bullshit* is less polite and more intense than *humbug*, there's no important difference between the two. But when *bullshit* was coined early in the twentieth century, it wasn't simply because people decided they needed a more emphatic way to say what's said by *humbug*. In fact the words are used rather differently: try substituting *humbug* or a more current term like *bunk* or *hogwash* in a sentence like "What a bullshit artist," "a totally bullshit assignment," or "Don't bullshit me!"

We already saw how the vulgarity of *asshole* shapes the various speech acts we perform with it—to insult, to disparage, to console. But the word's vulgarity colors its meaning in even more integral ways, just as the vulgarity of *bullshit* does. For one thing, we apply it only to people of our own sort. Osama bin Laden may have been "a thoroughly contemptible, detestable person," as *American Heritage* puts it, but you probably wouldn't describe him as an asshole even if you knew how badly he treated his subordinates and his wives. There's an intimacy to *asshole* and other vulgar words; nobody would contradict you if you said that Stalin was a shit, but that probably isn't how most of us would put the point. Vulgarity and meaning are inextricably bound or rather, there are ideas that only vulgar words can completely convey. *Asshole* doesn't just happen to have no respectable synonym: there couldn't be such a word.

chapter three

The Rise of Talking Dirty

Language in its primitive form is to be regarded as a mode of action rather than a countersign of thought.

> —**Bronisław Malinowski, "The Problem of Meaning in Primitive Languages," 1923**

Ma's out, pa's out, let's talk rude. Pee, poo, belly, bum, drawers!

> —**Michael Flanders and Donald Swann, "P★★, P★★, B★★★★, B★★, D★★★★★★"**

The Invention of the Asshole

The figure of the asshole made his literary debut in 1948 in Norman Mailer's *The Naked and the Dead*. That wasn't the very first published occurrence of *asshole* as a name for a disagreeable person: the word had appeared in passing in another war novel published three years earlier.* But Mailer was the first writer to attach the word to a fleshed-out character, in the person of Lieutenant Dove, a self-important naval officer seconded to an army unit on a South Pacific island during World War II. Dove is introduced with a description of Proustian precision:

> Lieutenant (sg) Dove, USNR. A Cornell man, a Deke, a perfect asshole. He was six feet two and weighed about a hundred and sixty pounds, with straight ash-blond hair cut close, and a clean pleasant vacuous face. . . . [Dove] had been assigned to the division as an interpreter at about the same time Hearn had come in, and with amazing, with startling naïveté he had announced to everyone that his rank was equivalent to captain in the Army, and that the responsibilities of a lieutenant sg were greater than those of a major or lieutenant colonel in the Army. He had told the officers this in officers' mess on Motome and had been loved accordingly.

By the time *asshole* appeared in print, it had undoubtedly been circulating in army slang for quite a while. In fact it doesn't really make sense to ask when this use of *asshole* was "coined." It isn't one of those items like *pizzazz* or *beatnik* that a clever columnist or copywriter can drop into the language some Tuesday morning. After all, it doesn't take a great deal of ingenuity to compare someone you want to disparage to the anus, and it's fair to assume that people have been do-

---

*Some slang dictionaries record earlier uses of the word from the 1930s, but in context those examples turn out to involve the anatomical meaning.

ing that from time to time for as long as *asshole* (or in its older form *arsehole*) has been around.

Still, it isn't likely that *asshole* was a conventional epithet much before the modern period. Even in more straight-laced ages, vulgarities and profanities show up in sources such as diaries, personal letters, pornography, slang dictionaries, and the records of prosecutions for public disorderliness or military insubordination ("Go and f— yourself" made its first print appearance in the proceedings of the Old Bailey in 1901). People have been using *arsehole* to refer to the anus at least since Chaucer's time, and there are citations from the 1860s on for the metaphorical use of the word for the most detestable spot in a region, as in "the arse-hole of the universe." So if *asshole* had been a routine term of abuse much before World War II, there would most likely be some record of it. Ernest Hemingway didn't use the word in the manuscript of *A Farewell to Arms* that he submitted to Scribner's in 1929, which included *shit, fuck, cocksucker, cunt*, and *balls*, none of which made it into the published version. That's not conclusive, of course, but if *asshole* had been around then, it's a fair bet Hemingway would have taken to it (it did show up in *Islands in the Stream*, written in the early 1950s and set during World War II).

So it almost certainly wasn't until the late 1930s or 1940s that *asshole* acquired the specific implications of self-importance and obtuseness that Mailer imputed to Lieutenant Dove. And even then, this meaning of the term wasn't well established outside of army slang. In his memoir *Doing Battle*, Paul Fussell recounts that as a college student waiting to be called up in 1942, he and his roommate invented an imaginary student named Philip Phallus:

Philip was a nerd—a chemistry major—who played the violin. . . . Waiting entailed other forms of idleness, like the hours I spent with Ed refining definitions—trying especially to specify the difference between an *asshole* and a *shit*, with examples drawn from male students of our acquaintance or our imagination. Philip Phallus was clearly an asshole, dumb, sincere, dull, and harmless.

At the time, apparently, Fussell thought of *asshole* as meaning something like the modern *dweeb* or *wuss*. It was only a few years later, as a junior officer in the European theater, that he cottoned to what was to become the common sense of the word. Forced to listen to "a vainglorious harangue" by General George S. Patton, he turned to the officer standing next to him and remarked sotto voce, "What an asshole!" by which presumably he didn't mean that Patton was sincere, dull or harmless.*

Asshole was a relative latecomer to the list of descriptive words that were derived from obscenities in this period. According to Lighter's *Historical Dictionary of American Slang*, the noun *fuck* for "a despicable person" was first recorded in 1927,

---

*The word is an anachronism in a scene in *The King's Speech* set in Westminster Abbey in 1936 during the preparation for the coronation of George VI, in which Geoffrey Rush as Lionel Logue makes a delightful pun that would unfortunately have made no sense at the time.

KING GEORGE VI: You can't sit there, get up.

LIONEL LOGUE: Why not? It's a chair.

KING GEORGE VI: No that is not a chair, that is St. Edward's chair. . . . That chair is the seat on which every king . . .

LIONEL LOGUE: I don't care how many royal assholes sat in this chair.

and the first unambiguous use of *cocksucker* as a general term of contempt appears in 1919 in a diary entry by John Dos Passos. And *prick* first shows up as a word for a vicious person in a 1927 letter of John O'Hara (its use as a term of affection for a man in Elizabethan times was long obsolete by then).

Those epithets were part of a larger vocabulary of words for various personal failings and social offenses that appeared in the first half of the twentieth century, all formed from a small set of time-honored scatological and sexual terms. *Bullshit* makes its first recorded appearance as a name for inflated humbug in a 1914 letter from Ezra Pound to James Joyce—T. S. Eliot wrote a poem called "The Triumph of Bullshit" in 1910, but it wasn't published until a few years later. *Chickenshit* first appears in the sense "contemptible or worthless" in a Hemingway letter of 1936 and in the sense "niggling or trivial" in a Dos Passos diary reference to "the little chickenshit attitudes of a bright student in a girl's college." *Fuck around* in the sense "play around; to waste time" first shows up in a 1931 letter of Henry Miller, whose *Tropic of Cancer* also provides the first recorded instance of the verb *shit* in the sense "attempt to deceive."

It isn't surprising that so many of these new words made their first recorded appearances in the diaries and letters of modernist writers, which are among the few unexpurgated records of the colloquial language of that period that have come down to us. But the expressions weren't the coinings of the avant-garde. They were working-class inventions that Pound, Eliot, Dos Passos, and the others took up in their capacity as literary bad boys, an embrace of popular vulgarity being a useful way of demonstrating one's contempt for bourgeois conventionality. (In a 1919 letter, E. E. Cummings described *bullshit* as "a forte and accurate expression-du-peuple.")

The hand of the working class in creating the new vocabulary is more directly evident by the time we get to the spate of new items that appeared around the time of the Second World War, many of which were documented by war novelists who took advantage of the wider linguistic latitude that publishers were permitting them. That's when we encounter the first recorded uses of *pissed off* for angry, *get on someone's ass* for harass or pester, *ballbreaker* for a difficult task or exigent taskmaster, *fuck up* for a misfit or chronic bumbler, *fuck with* to mean meddle or interfere, and *fuck off* for shirk or loaf. (*The Naked and the Dead* also provides the first written appearance of the noun *fuck off*—or as Mailer's publisher obliged him to spell it, *fug off*—as well as the first sighting of the alternative *dick off*.)

Many of these expressions were probably floating around in soldiers' slang for quite a while. But it was the war that gave them their point of entry into the wider American vocabulary, as draftees from a range of backgrounds were proletarianized for the duration and subjected to the unrelenting regime of petty harassment and mindless bureaucratic rigmarole that passed under the heading of chickenshit. In an essay on the pervasiveness of chickenshit in the World War II military, Fussell notes how vulgarity expressed all of the rancor and antipathy stirred up by the military class war:

> Indispensable both to those administering chickenshit and those receiving it, *fucking* helped express the resentment of both sides, the one resenting the constant frustration of its

authority, the other resenting its constant victimhood. Among the working class *fucking* had always been a popular intensifier, but in wartime it became precious as a way for millions of conscripts to note, in a licensed way, their bitterness and anger. If you couldn't oppose the chickenshit in any other way, you could always say, "Fuck it!"

Of course swearing has been the privileged recourse of the Other Ranks for as long as there have been armies. ("She curses and storms at me like a Trooper," Samuel Richardson wrote in 1740, the first recorded instance of what became a stock figure of speech.) What was new was both the social diversity of the participants and the vocabulary it made use of.

As Fussell's observations remind us, the creation of new meanings for *asshole, fuck up*, and *pissed off* and the rest paralleled the conversion of obscene words into new intensifiers and interjections. *Fucking* made its first appearance as a quasi-adjective in the late nineteenth century in phrases like "my fucking boots" (it was first recorded in Farmer and Henley's 1890 *Dictionary of Slang and Its Analogues*, which defined it aseptically as "an expression of extreme contumely"). The word soon acquired a remarkable syntactic versatility. "The world is too fucking with us," Pound wrote in 1918, using the word as a quasi-adverb, while World War I doughboys turned it into an infix, as in "Armen-fucking-teers" for Armentières.★ And by the early decades of the twentieth century, *fuck* was

---

★I say "quasi-adjective" and "quasi-adverb" because these items don't really behave like ordinary adjectives and adverbs. *Fucking* in "the fucking car" may seem to be parallel to *red* or *old*, but we can't say "How fucking was the car?" or "The car

replacing the profanities *damn* and *hell* in phrases like *what the fuck, fuck if I know*, and *fucking well*, not to mention *fuck you*, which was first recorded in 1909. The transition is reflected in the evolution of a World War I joke about a soldier who is having his first dinner at home after several years at the front and asks his mother, "Goddamn it, Ma, where in hell's the butter?" In the World War II version, the soldier's request was revised to "Where's the fucking butter?"

The Twilight of Profanity

Those substitutions signaled a dramatic change in the raw material of swearing. Our loose use of *profanity* as a synonym for "swear word" is a legacy of the Victorian era, when swearing consisted almost entirely of profanity in its narrow sense: oaths involving *damn, Lord, God, Jesus, Christ*, and above all *hell*, a word that nineteenth-century Americans were famous for using with a dazzling virtuosity: *a hell of a drink, what in hell?, give him hell, the hell I will, go to hell*, and countless others. To the Victorians, those imprecations were noisome enough to spawn a whole vocabulary of the substitutes that H. L. Mencken called "denaturized profanities" including *heck, goldarn, doggone, dadburned, tarnation, gee-whiz, all-fired, blazes*, and the like. Mencken dismissed such words as "by the Y.W.C.A. out of the tea-shoppe," but they sounded stronger

---

looked fucking." And while you can say "That dessert was fucking good," if someone asks "How good was the dessert?" you can't just say "Fucking," though you could answer "Very."

to Victorian ears and had little of the comical overtones that they have for us.★ To reckon by the schedule of fines for cursing posted in a World War I military hospital, *goldarn* at 15¢ was considered stronger than a plain *damn* at 10¢ but less culpable than a "*damn* with an extra"—*goddamn*? *double-damn*?—which would set the offender back a quarter.

But Victorian profanity was never really intended as blasphemous, other than incidentally. For honest-to-God blasphemy—"evil speaking against God maliciously," as Milton defined it—you have to go to the popular traditions of Catholic cultures, like the Italian oaths called *bestemmie*: *porco Dio*, "pig God," *madonna troia,* "whore madonna," and so on. Rather, the profanity was a working-class response to the condescending sanctimoniousness of the ruling orders: "the response that recklessness makes to hypocrisy," in the words of the Unitarian preacher Octavius Brooks Frothingham. "The profanity of the streets," Frothingham wrote in 1876,

> is certainly disgusting enough to the refined taste, but it is less impious than it sounds. The people who indulge in loud and frequent oaths do so for the most part thoughtlessly ... "God" is a term oftenest in the mouths of people who repel them

---

★When HBO premiered its series *Deadwood,* set in a South Dakota mining camp in the 1870s, critics noted that its language was extreme even by the standards of pay cable. In every scene, characters were saying "what the fuck," "who gives a fuck," "who's that ugly fuck," and "shit out of luck." Actually, none of those words would have been used at the time. Even the roughest of the roughnecks back then would have gone no further than *goddamn* or *son of a bitch*—though the latter could still be inflected with its literal meaning, as indicated by the famous line from Owen Wister's 1902 Western novel *The Virginian*: "When you call me that, smile."

by their solemn faces and sanctimonious manners. . . . For the common profanity of men the pious people of the community are responsible to a larger degree than they suspect.

Frothingham probably exaggerated the theological ignorance of the people he described as "the low-lived and vicious," but he understood the motive for their profanity. Like the swearing of soldiers in World War II, the point was to demonstrate a contempt for the proprieties dictated by the officer class, whether military or civilian. Ellen Bayuk Rosenman describes the vulgarity of the Victorian working class as a kind of tax evasion, "a protest against . . . bourgeois standards and a defense of their own territories, customs, and traditions."

Working-class vulgarity wasn't like the cant or slang of the working-class or the underworld, which served to mark an in-group status or to conceal what was being said from the casual listener. (Thackeray parodied the cant in *Vanity Fair*: "Is that your snum? I'll gully the dag and bimbole the clicky in a snuffkin.") Swear words had to be readily comprehensible to outsiders, so that they could be shocked by them. For those purposes, it wasn't terribly important whether the transgression involved the use of religious language in low contexts or the mention of obscene terms, which made the transition from profanity to obscenity nearly seamless: when the former became less scandalous, soldiers naturally reached for the latter.

What mattered was the effect the words would have on superiors, authorities, or simply the "respectable," whether or not they were actually present. The soldier's pleasure in saying "goddamn" or later "fucking" arose from imagining the indignation the language would evoke, or in imagining being able to say the words to an officer's face with impunity. Paul Fussell recounts a "rumor-joke" popular among enlisted men in the European Theater that gave expression to every soldier's fantasies of insubordination: General Patton, inspecting a hospital in France, chews out a man for not coming to attention in his presence. The man replies, "Run along, asshole—I'm in the merchant marine." The joke has a modern successor in the story about the Texan who's visiting Harvard (with variants about an American asking a Londoner how to find Big Ben, etc.):

> TEXAN: Where's the library at?
> PROFESSOR: Here at Hahvahd we don't end our
>   sentences with a preposition.
> TEXAN: OK, then, where's the library at, asshole?

As in the World War II joke, *asshole* is the rejoinder of the ordinary Joe to pretension or self-importance, the difference being that in the contemporary version the speaker doesn't have to justify his right to be impertinent.

Now as then, the subtext of swearing has always been class. In 1901, Professor G. T. W. Patrick wrote in *Psychological Review* that swearing was particularly prevalent "among soldiers and sailors, in the laboring classes, among the uneducated, and among criminals," who had not understood that "advancing civilization bids us evermore inhibit and repress." But swearing was never restricted to the lower orders. Rather, those associations gave it its potency for middle-class speakers, who have always used it to evoke the traits that custom assigns to working-class men—to make themselves sound tough, forthright, and intolerant of pretension and prudishness, particularly in those all-male contexts where the use of bad words is ritualized. The upper-class "dandies" who joined Teddy Roosevelt's Rough Riders in Cuba proved to be, to the surprise of the regular army soldiers in the unit, "a husky lot of fellers . . . they was expert on the swear."

By the early twentieth century though, the taboos were fraying. Swearing was becoming common, even in smart middle-class social settings and in mixed company. From the First World War onwards, we run into frequent denunciations of the fashionable use of swear words by would-be sophisticates, a vogue derided as the "mucker pose." That phrase was first popularized in a 1921 article in *Harper's* by the novelist Philip Curtiss, who defined it as "that curious state of mind which induces well-bred, intelligent people to disclaim superciliously any refinement, education, or natural good taste which heredity or opportunity may have given them, and to set themselves deliberately to the worship of the coarse and the commonplace." Writing in the same magazine a few years later, the historian James Truslow Adams wrote that the mucker-poseurs "do not content themselves with talking like uneducated half-wits. They also emulate the language and manners of the bargee and the longshoreman . . . and assume as protective coloration the manners and thought level of those who are beneath them." He cited the "young scion of American aristocracy with every social and educational advantage" describing his new position in banking to friends at his club as "the God-damnedest most interesting job in the world."

Nor was the use of risqué language the exclusive province of men: "If one wants to acquire an extensive and varied vocabulary of the most modern sort," Adams said, "one has merely to watch the young ladies of the mucker-poseur type playing tennis at Southhampton or Newport." Writing in *Harper's* in 1927, Mary Agnes Hamilton noted that anyone who listened to modern conversation would be struck by the "high proportion, in that vocabulary, of words such as, in the older jargon, 'no lady could use,'" in particular the "expletives and 'swear words' that have no real significance in this unbelieving age. They are all over the place; they act as a sort of obbligato to a modern conversation." The point was illustrated by a drawing from a 1931 book called *The Deb's Dictionary* that defined *damn* as "a feminine expression of annoyance."

Ordinary middle-class Americans were slower to adjust to the more permissive climate, and many of the official sanctions on profanity remained in place for a long time. As late as mid-century, a number of American newspapers hesitated to use even softened profanities such as *damfool* and *helluva*, while the Hays Code prohibited the appearance in movies of items like *God*, *Lord*, and *Jesus Christ* "unless used reverently." When he made *Gone with the Wind* in 1939, David Selznick happily paid a $5,000 fine for the privilege of including Rhett Butler's closing "Frankly, my dear, I don't give a damn." But as profanity became more common in literature and the theater it inevitably lost a lot of its shock value. As Hamilton wrote, "Playwrights are out to shock audiences who, as a matter of fact, are immune to the kind of shock they seek to give them. . . . Dramatists thoroughly involved in the effort to do 'strong' things get 'stronger' and 'stronger'; their audience's reaction gets weaker and weaker." When the World War I drama *What Price Glory* opened on Broadway in 1924, a story went the rounds about a young man who took his elderly aunt to see the play, unaware that it was laced with soldierly profanities. Increasingly uncomfortable on her behalf, he suggested at the end of act one that they leave, to which she replied, "Just let me find my goddamned handkerchief."

The enfeeblement of profanity led some to predict the disappearance of swearing. The critic Burges Johnson wrote in 1931: "When man began to lose his belief in a petty-minded, interfering God, then oaths and curses began to lose their true value . . . [Now] even the surviving cuss-words, maledictions, and execrations of ancient and half-forgotten lineage are dying of anemia, sharing the fate of *zounds* and *gramercy* and *odsblood*." And H. L. Mencken wrote in 1944 that "all recent writers upon the subject seem to be agreed that profanity is now in one of its periods of waning." That was the very same perception that stimulated the coining of obscene counterparts for profanities among the working class, as we saw, and these too were soon being picked up by middle-class sophisticates, led by avant-garde writers like Dos Passos and Pound. Denatured obscenities like "freaking" for *fucking* entered the language in the 1920s, an indication that people were feeling the need to suggest the word without actually saying it. So, too, did the phrase "dirty word" in its modern meaning as an obscenity.*

---

*Before the 1920s a dirty word was simply one that was disreputable or disparaging; in the *OED*'s first cited example for the phrase, from 1842, a Catholic cook says, "Don't say popery, it's a dirty word! Say Roman Catholic when you speak of the faith."

Vulgarity in Mufti

It was some time before the secondhand obscenities would enter the register of general middle-class speech. At first, the language that the discharged GIs brought back with them struck many as an incomprehensible register. Mencken may have lamented the weakening of profanities, he but took no solace in the appearance of their obscene counterparts; writing in 1948, he said:

> We have lately seen the heroes of a great moral war march home with a repertory of invective almost tragically thin and banal. Like any other Christian soldiers, they used a great deal of foul language in field and camp, but very little of it got beyond a few four-letter words. These four-letter words were so cruelly overworked that . . . they came to mean anything or everything. A soldier simply threw in one or another of them whenever his flow of ideas began to run sluggish, which was usually.

When *The Naked and the Dead* came out in that same year, many critics saw its language not just as repugnant but as alien. Orville Prescott gave the novel a rave review in the *New York Times* ("the most impressive novel about the second World War that I have ever read"), but took Mailer to task for his excessive use of obscenities:

> In his effort to carry his realistic portrayal of men at war to the ultimate degree of authenticity he has wallowed in a

grotesque and exaggerated fidelity to the coarseness of their language. In the middle of this outspoken century no normal adult has any illusions about the profanity and obscenity of soldier talk. But . . . there is more explicitly vile speech in "The Naked and the Dead" than I have ever seen printed in a work of serious literature before. It is probably truthful reporting, but it is unnecessarily offensive and it is marvelously tiresome.

More than sixty years later, what strikes us as quaint about that passage isn't just Prescott's prim disapproval of Mailer's more or less faithful rendering of his characters' language. It's also Prescott's assumption that the language belonged to an exotic dialect of "soldier talk" and his conjecture that the reporting was "probably" truthful, as if he were evaluating the accuracy of nautical terminology in a Patrick O'Brian novel set during the Napoleonic Wars.

Even as Prescott was writing, though, the new vocabulary was becoming more commonplace in sophisticated circles. War novelists such as Mailer, James Jones, Leon Uris, and Irwin Shaw may have had something to do with that, as did the Beats and the writers of noir fiction. In the postwar period, one British publisher noted, a measure of forbidden language was "almost obligatory in any novel that laid claims to realism." Indeed, by the time Herman Wouk's *The Caine Mutiny* was published in 1951, it was noteworthy for its linguistic restraint—in an explanatory note, Wouk said that he had left unrecorded "the general obscenity and blasphemy of shipboard talk . . . which is largely monotonous." By then,

Wouk's reticence was so unusual that *Time* headed its review of the book "Realism Without Obscenity."*

But the new language was chiefly spread by the returning servicemen themselves. During the war, Bernard DeVoto noted in 1948, "military life made most of the monosyllables automatic in the conversation of the soldiers and sailors whom millions of women knew," even as the taboo on the use of the words in mixed company was being relaxed. Indeed, he noted, among well-to-do and metropolitan women, four-letter words were coming to signify "frankness, sophistication, liberalism, companionability, and even smartness." DeVoto suggested that the appearance of the words in recent fiction merely reflected their growing acceptability in speech: "Literature lags behind society, and this change was well established before fiction took much note of it. On the upper level of society the words have lost much of the shocking power in conversation that they used to have, and since those are the levels which read fiction, they have therefore lost most of their shocking power in print." He went on to observe that it is the people who do not commonly read novels who are most distressed at seeing the words in books.

But the habits of metropolitan sophisticates of DeVoto's circles in Cambridge and New York weren't representative of the general drift of American speech. On the contrary, the very fact that an occasional use of the four-letter words was considered "smart" suggests that they were still considered

---

*Wouk could play his reticence about setting down the sailors' billingsgate to comic advantage: "Bellison uncorked a flood of horrible profanity, which, translated, meant 'This is extremely unusual.'"

daring or naughty, and that this was an advanced form of elite mucker-posing, not yet part of middle-class speech or even prep-school slang. Holden Caulfield's swearing in Salinger's 1950 *The Catcher in the Rye* is largely restricted to profanities like *goddam* and *hell*, and an occasional *Chrissake* when angry; his obscenities go no further than *ass* and *crap*. When he does encounter *fuck you* written on the wall of his sister's school, he's distressed by it:

> But while I was sitting down, I saw something that drove me crazy. Somebody'd written "Fuck you" on the wall. It drove me damn near crazy. I thought how Phoebe and all the other little kids would see it, and how they'd wonder what the hell it meant, and then finally some dirty kid would tell them— all cockeyed, naturally—what it meant, and how they'd all think about it and maybe even worry about it for a couple of days. I kept wanting to kill whoever'd written it.

True, Holden might very well have used the expression himself in another context if he was sufficiently provoked (though it's easier to imagine it coming from Ackley or Stradlater). Still, Salinger didn't have Holden use *fucking* as an intensifier or say *pissed off, fuck up, no shit, fuck around* or other items that would have been routine in the speech of adolescents a generation later—and he didn't use *asshole*, though the word would have applied perfectly to half the characters in the novel if it had been part of Holden's active vocabulary. That clearly wasn't out of Salinger's sense of delicacy, given that he had no qualms about including the *fuck you*'s that kept the book on most-frequently-banned lists for the next thirty years. At the time, upper-middle-class adolescent boys didn't yet talk that way. A few years later, things would be different. By the mid-fifties John O'Hara's brittle upper-class women characters are saying things like "You're damn fucking right I am" and "I feel like a shit" (though *asshole* doesn't appear in any of his novels). By then, Holden would have been saying them, too.

The Repeal of Reticence

It's natural to see the spread and acceptance of the new vocabulary as another episode in "the repeal of reticence," the name the historian Rachel Gurstein has given to the century-long process in which society abandoned Victorian inhibitions about the public discussion of sexuality, the body, and the intimate details of personal life. The phrase originated as the title of an article by the Catholic writer Agnes Repplier that sparked a national discussion when it appeared in 1914 in the *Atlantic Monthly*. Repplier sounded an alarm about the books, plays, and articles about sex that were flooding America, and complained about the breaking of the "obsession of sex which has set us all a-babbling about matters once excluded from the amenities of conversation":

> Stories minutely describing houses of ill-fame, their furniture, their food, their barred windows, their perfumed air, and the men with melancholy eyes who visit them. Novels purporting to be candid and valuable studies of degeneracy and nymphomania. . . . All these horrors, which would have made

honest old Hogarth turn uneasily in his grave, are offered for the defense of youth and purifying of civilized society.

Those "horrors" were all productions of what Gurstein calls "the party of exposure." Its program was played out in the high cultural world of the artistic and social movements that culminated in the counterculture, the New Left, the "sexual revolution," women's liberation, and gay liberation, all of them pressing for an end to the social and legal impediments to frank expression. It brings to mind D. H. Lawrence and Henry Miller, Allen Ginsberg and William S. Burroughs, Margaret Sanger and Margaret Meade, Albert Ellis and Alfred Kinsey, Jerry Rubin and Lenny Bruce, *Oh Calcutta!* and *Fear of Flying*, and all the other modernist and avant-garde assaults on Victorian sexual neuroses. As Lawrence explained in "A Propos of 'Lady Chatterley's Lover,'" published in 1930, he had used "taboo words" because "we shall never free the phallic reality from the 'uplift' taint till we give it its own phallic language."★

But the story is very different when it comes to the secondhand vulgarities, *asshole* among them. Their appearance and spread had little to do with dispelling the shame attached to the body and its functions. On the contrary, it's only because *asshole* is considered a dirty word when it's used anatomically that it can convey contempt when it's applied to an office martinet or an inconsiderate motorist. Hemingway,

---

★The word *taboo* had been in the language since the time of Captain Cook, but it was chiefly associated with the superstitions of Polynesians and other primitive societies. The modernists were the first to use it to suggest the primitive irrationality of Victorian interdictions on speaking frankly about sex.

Mailer, and Jones weren't interested in sanitizing *fuck* or *asshole* into cheerfully anodyne descriptions; rather the use of the words was offered as naturalistic depictions of the language of soldiers, criminals, or the working class in all its gritty reality. In his 1933 decision exonerating *Ulysses* from the charge of obscenity, Judge John Woolsey justified Joyce's use of objectionable words by observing that such language "would be naturally and habitually used . . . by the types of folk whose life, physical and mental, Joyce is seeking to describe."

But, as different as the literal and figurative uses of these words are, most people have trouble keeping them distinct. That's understandable, since the literal meanings of words like *fucking* and *asshole* continue to taint them even when they're used figuratively or as epithets.★ Hence the controversy that began in 2003 when the FCC declined to sanction NBC for indecency after Bono uttered the F-word on the Golden Globe awards broadcast, saying, "This is really, really, fucking brilliant." The agency staffers noted that their guidelines limited indecency to "material that describes or depicts sexual or excretory organs or activities," whereas Bono, they pointed out correctly, had merely used the word as "an expletive to emphasize an exclamation." A few months later, not long after Janet Jackson's Super Bowl "wardrobe malfunction," the com-

---

★It's true children often learn the figurative or epithetical uses of these words before learning their unsavory literal meanings, if ever they do—think of *douchebag*—but here I think they simply assume there must be some salacious meaning to the word. By and large, it's rare to find vulgar epithets derived from words that have inoffensive literal meanings or no literal meaning at all (as in "Splack! What a sycamore waste of time!"). It sometimes happens, though, that a word retains its vulgarity after the connection to the literal meaning is lost, as most notably with *bloody*.

mission reversed itself, stating that "given the core meaning of the 'F-Word,' any use of that word or a variation, in any context, inherently has a sexual connotation, and therefore falls within the first prong of our indecency definition." But there's a difference between what a word connotes and what it "describes or depicts," as the legal definition of indecency puts it. *Mouse* may bring to mind a furry rodent when it refers to a computer pointing device, but it doesn't depict one. That was the point implied by the New York Court of Appeals when it overturned the FCC's judgment, pointing out that "fleeting expletives" like Bono's *fucking* had no sexual meaning, so couldn't be indecent in the legal sense of the term. The subtleties of these distinctions were lost on the Republican FCC chairman, Kevin Martin, who said in response, "I find it hard to believe that the New York court would tell American families that 'shit' and 'fuck' are fine to say on broadcast television . . . The New York court is divorced from reality in concluding that the word 'fuck' does not invoke a sexual connotation."*

The agency's critics had a lot of fun with that position, in the course of things blurring the distinction between connotation and meaning themselves. The political blogger Daniel Drezner asked, "If I say 'F#$% Kevin Martin and the horse he rode in on,' am I obviously encouraging rape and bestiality?" But if "fucking brilliant" obviously doesn't *describe* sexual activity and for that reason can't be legally indecent, it doesn't

---

*It's a telling sign of how standards have evolved that Martin managed to repeat *shit* and *fuck* half a dozen times in the course of five short paragraphs condemning the court's decision—not something you could imagine coming from an FCC chairman from some earlier era. Traditionalist or no, Martin is clearly not a man who has much use for old-fashioned demurrals like "decency forbids me."

follow that it has no lubricious overtones. If a word is dirty when it's used literally, then it's dirty when it's used figuratively or as an expletive—though that's hardly a reason for banning it from the airwaves.

As Martin's statement suggests, people on both sides of the debates over explicitness have often had a political interest in suppressing the differences between the literal and figurative uses of these words. In the 1960s, some on the left incorporated sexual liberation into their political program and tried to attach a revolutionary significance to the use of sexually explicit language. As Jerry Rubin put it:

> There's one word which Amerika hasn't destroyed. One word which has maintained its emotional power and purity. Amerika cannot destroy it because she dare not use it. It's illegal! It's the last word left in the English language: FUCK!
>
> The naked human body is immoral under Christianity and illegal under Amerikan law. Nudity is called "indecent exposure." Fuck is a dirty word because you have to be naked to do it.

Rubin went on to praise the Berkeley protestors who wrote "FUCK WAR" on a piece of cardboard and got arrested, giving birth to the Filthy Speech Movement in 1965. In the process he neatly elided the differences between the literal and figurative meanings of *fuck*, leaving it unclear why, if sex ought to be pure and wholesome, you would wish it on the things you revile.

To be sure, that was a minority view on the left. While the Filthy Speech Movement got a lot of media attention at the time, it was regarded as an annoying distraction by the leaders of the Free Speech Movement that engendered it; in a speech, Mario Savio couldn't even bring himself to refer to a "Fuck" sign as other than "the sexual intercourse sign," and indignantly denied that the FSM had anything to do with "the unfortunate sexual intercourse movement." But others insisted that the two issues were intrinsically connected. Rubin would later write, "The Free Speech Movement was raped in the same bed with the Filthy Speech Movement. . . . It was an early sign of the split between political radicals and the hippie/yippies. How can you separate politics from sex? It's all the same thing. . . . Puritanism leads us to Vietnam." It was a presage of the seventies, when sexual and personal liberation were disconnected from political activism—and when Rubin himself would wind up as an acolyte of est.

But however dubious the logic of equating the sexual and expletive uses of *fuck,* the word is unambiguous in its challenge to authority. As the Students for a Democratic Society leader Mark Rudd explained in 1970 in the Marxoid jargon of the movement, the use of shocking language "had the advantage of selectively targeting established population elements: in addition to social-class differentials, young people did not find crude language as offensive as did older ones." Within a few years shock language had become an audible stylistic trait of the movement and the counterculture in general. In a memorable scene from the movie *Woodstock*, Country Joe McDonald introduced his anti-war anthem "Feel Like I'm Fixin' to Die Rag" with a call-and-response: "Give me an F . . . Give me a U . . . Give me a C . . . Give me a K . . . What's that spell? WHAT'S THAT SPELL?" It was a connection between the sexual and the political that Lenny Bruce had summed up succinctly a few years earlier: "Take away the right to say *fuck* and you take away the right to say fuck the government."

The Rediscovery of Civility

The defenders of the established order had their own reasons for linking the literal and figurative meanings of these words. The counterculture's penchant for using obscenities made it easy to link the promiscuity, drug use, and unkempt personal appearance of the youth with their radicalism and their contempt for traditional values (another phrase that worked its way into political language around this time). Their critics contended, not without reason, that the sorts of people who would speak freely about fucking were exactly the sorts who would yell "Fuck you!" at the representatives of authority. After Mayor Daley's police attacked demonstrators outside the 1968 Democratic Convention in Chicago, the eventual nominee, Hubert Humphrey, justified their actions by saying, "The obscenity, the profanity, the filth that was uttered night after night in front of the hotels was an insult to every woman, every mother, every daughter, indeed, every human being. . . . You'd put anybody in jail for that kind of talk."

The desire to connect the demonstrators' personal behavior and political views had notable linguistic consequence, one curiously connected to the adoption of *asshole*. It provided the motive for reintroducing the notion of "civility" into public life, setting in motion the politicization of personal life that would become a signal feature of the era. People today invariably speak of civility as an antique and eternal virtue—the assumption you have to make about any virtue if you're going to go on to perceive a decline in it. It's true that the words *civility* and *incivility* themselves go back to the Renaissance, and modern writers often take them back still further, pointing out that *civility* is derived from the Latin word for city and related to *civilization*. George Will's explanation is typical: "Manners are the practice of a virtue. The virtue is called civility, a word related—as a foundation is related to a house—to the word civilization."

But whatever their remote etymologies, the connection of *civility* and *incivility* to public life was lost sight of several hundred years ago. To Victorians, *incivility* suggested merely an impertinent coachman or a stall-keeper who addressed one as "boss" rather than "sir." Writing in 1839, Thomas De Quincey ranked it as a vice that fell somewhere between procrastination and Sabbath-breaking on a scale of gravity. By the early twentieth century *civility* was merely a genteel term for a formally correct courtesy. When Westbrook Pegler wrote dismissively of the "civility" of the newly elected President Franklin Roosevelt in 1933, he was referring not to the president's relations with the press or the Republican opposition but to his "suburban neighborliness" in calling the grocery boy by name. As late as the 1950s, critics writing about serious social concerns like juvenile delinquency spoke about a "breakdown of manners and morals"; *incivility* didn't come into the picture. Indeed, when philosophers and social theorists began to revive *civility* in the 1950s and 1960s to stress the importance of rational and respectful debate in a democratic society, they acknowledged that this sense of the word was effectively obsolete. In 1958, the sociologist Edward Shils complained that "it is an impoverishment of our thought on political matters that this word has been allowed to dwindle to the point where it has come to refer to good manners in face-to-face relationships," and lamented that recent books on civility by Sir Ernest Barker and Sir Harold Nicholson showed no awareness that the term had ever suggested anything more than urbane courtesy.

When commentators and social critics disinterred *civility* and *incivility* in the 1960s, it was with a specific political purpose in mind. In their eyes, the social upheavals personified by the hippies, anti-war protesters, and campus radicals offered provocations that transcended mere breaches of decorum or anything that could be conveyed by pallid old words like *impolite, rude*, and *discourteous*. With its musty connection to *citizen* and *civic*, a resuscitated *incivility* implied that the demonstrators' dress and rude comportment was of a piece with their attacks on the political order. In an editorial that appeared just before the 1968 elections, the *Wall Street Journal* inveighed against what it called the New Incivility, whose perpetrators included the student protesters whose "foul mouth ranting made a disgusting mockery of political discourse," the "filthy hecklers who dogged the steps of presidential candidate Hubert Humphrey," and the "enraged Negro spokesmen" who "denied any virtue in white civilization." The offense of the hippies and protestors didn't lie just in what they were saying, but in their repugnant personal habits and physical appearance. With their slovenly hair and beards and their deliberate squalor, the *Journal* said, they were showing their "rejection of and contempt for the world of decent manners," and were assaulting "not only a political system but the dignity of the individual and human life itself." Within a few years, the *Journal* had extended the charge of incivility to communes—"pigsties, literally and morally"—and to "ultramilitant feminists who blur distinctions and appear bent on creating animosities where none existed." As the *Journal*'s editorialists put it, "In an age racked by violence it may seem trivial indeed to speak of the decline of manners. Yet that falling-off is symptomatic of a concurrent decline of tolerance and hence has something to do with the violence itself." The connection the critics made between the radicals' politics and their uninhibited language helped establish a persistent assumption that the modern upsurge of vulgarity was rooted in the counterculture and left-wing rage.★

At the time, though, the liberal establishment was no less alarmed by the tenor and language of the sixties movements, particularly on campus. In an effort to be even-handed, the *New York Times* acknowledged the short-sightedness of university leadership, but nonetheless declared that the protesters were "contemptuous . . . of the basic rules of civility." In 1969 alone, *civility* and *incivility* appeared in more *Times* editorials than they had in the previous half-century, almost all of them dealing with campus turbulence. In subsequent years, the

---

★In 2007, when a conservative blog posted a study—as it happens, statistically meaningless—that purported to show that George Carlin's infamous "seven dirty words" appeared more often in the top liberal blogs than the top conservative ones, the syndicated conservative columnist Mona Charen took the result as confirming that the left is responsible for an "explosion of vulgarity, cruelty, and viciousness" on the web.

Times extended the words to cover both inner-city riots and cross-burnings and the everyday courtesies expected between people waiting in line for movies. By the Clinton years, the words were fifteen times as frequent in the press as they had been during Eisenhower's presidency; in 2004, one dictionary website picked *incivility* as word of the year, ahead of *blogosphere*, *flip-flop*, and *Red States/Blue States*.

It's not a coincidence that the new sense of *incivility* emerged at the same time that *asshole* came of age as a reproach for social misconduct. True, the words entered the language from opposite directions: the reinvented *incivility* was the conscious creation of social critics and polemicists, while *asshole* bubbled up from working-class slang. But *civility* and *incivility*, like *asshole*, were a response to the cultural upheavals of the moment, and presumed the same rejection of traditional values. For all that people invariably speak of civility as an abiding virtue, in its new guise it's actually a sharp break with the past. To evoke civility is to presuppose that old-fashioned manners and politeness aren't morally compelling by themselves, a point writers invariably acknowledge in the way they define the notion:

Civility is more than mere politeness or courtesy; it is an active consideration of others in one's actions and thoughts.

Intellectual civility is not a matter of mere courtesy, but arises from a sense that communication itself requires honoring others' views . . .

Don't let people confuse civility with goody two-shoes niceness and mere etiquette. Civility is a robust, tough, substantive civic virtue.

The giveaway here isn't "more than" but "mere." It's fair to say civility isn't reducible to politeness or manners, but social critics in other times would have been disconcerted to hear moralists disparaging the latter. An age in which even moralists can speak of "mere manners" and "mere courtesy" is very different from the one that preceded it, despite the specious continuity of values that "civility" is supposed to provide. The reinvention of *civility* and *incivility* implicitly conceded that authenticity and honesty took precedence over artifice, simulation, or "goody two-shoes niceness and mere etiquette"—a conception of social virtue that was more in sync with the sensibilities that took root in the sixties and seventies than with those of the Eisenhower years.★ But this is an age, after all, when America's best-known etiquette advisor calls herself Miss Manners and wears a camped-up high lace collar to preemptively neutralize the precious stereotypes that "manners" and "etiquette" can evoke. Indeed, the civilitarians' persistent references to "mere manners" convey exactly the same dismissive view of the conventional rules of decorum that the sarcastic "Mind your manners, asshole" does.

But there the resemblance between *incivility* and *asshole* fades. The words are different not just in the company they keep, but in their breadth of application. The point of *incivility* is to span the distinction between the private and the political and to blur the lines between moral categories. That's how

---

★One telling sign of how the meaning of *civility* had changed is that even as the word was being more and more widely used after the 1960s, there was a precipitous drop off in the use of the plural *civilities*, which was still associated with the older sense of formulaic and insincere politeness.

the word comes by its remarkable expansiveness, where it can apply to anything from failing to refill the photocopier tray to burning a Koran or describing a political opponent with a racist or ethnic slur. As the philosopher Cheshire Calhoun has pointed out, *incivility* is different from the name of any other vice in being "universally applicable to virtually any example of moral or mannerly misbehavior." By contrast, *asshole* signals in its very form that it shouldn't be used in polite discourse and that it should refer only to the perpetrators of slights that occur in the course of personal interaction, whether cutting into the left-turn lane or speaking abusively to an employee. Indeed, the way you turn your political adversaries into assholes is by subordinating their political views to their personal defects: depicting liberals as effete snobs or conservatives as heartless louts.

Above all, the words tell different stories. The reinvention of incivility was part of a conscious effort to give a political meaning to the cultural changes of the era. Whereas when *asshole* entered our everyday moral vocabulary, it was as an organic process which had less to do with the political agitation and ferment of the sixties than with the decade's stylistic innovation—and which in the end, among many other things, reduced much of politics to a form of cultural play.

chapter four

The Asshole
Comes of Age

*The surest sign that a group or society has entered into
the self-conscious possession of a new concept is that a
corresponding vocabulary will be developed, a vocabulary
which can then be used to pick out and discuss the concept
with consistency.*

—Quentin Skinner, "Language and Social Change"

*I don't know if you can be authentic if you are not out there
being authentic.*

—Rick Santorum

Naturalizing the Asshole

We all knew the word *asshole* when I was an undergraduate
in the early 1960s. I didn't use it very often, and it struck me
as stronger and more brazen then than it does today. (I recall

one guy I knew who used it a lot who I thought was pretty cool.) When it became a favorite epithet of the movement left a few years later, it was assuredly one of the items the editors of the *Wall Street Journal* had in mind when they castigated "foul-mouth demonstrators." In October of 1968, a group of SDS members from Kent State disrupted a Nixon rally in Akron with cries of "you fucking asshole" and "Sieg heil!" (Paraphrasing Bob Dylan, one SDS chapter used the slogan "You don't need a rectal thermometer to know who the assholes are," a vivid metaphor if you don't think it through.)

But for the movement, *asshole* was mostly a general term of contempt that was chosen because it made so many people uncomfortable and permitted the mostly middle-class radicals to lay claim to proletarian bona fides. Nixon (who was himself fond of the word), may very well have been an asshole, though to my mind he was something darker and weirder than that. But the point of calling him a fucking asshole wasn't to distinguish him from a prick or shit or bastard.★ It was meant simply as an insult, just as it was when SDS's Mark Rudd described Columbia's president Grayson Kirk as an asshole in a 1968 speech. At the time the phrase sounded theatrically insolent, like the tone Rudd took in his letter to "Uncle Grayson," which concluded: "I'll use the words of

---

★Cf. Frank Zappa's "Dickie's Such an Asshole," 1974:

The man in the white house—oooh!
He's got a conscience black as sin!
There's just one thing I wanna know—
How'd that asshole ever manage to get in?

LeRoi Jones, whom I'm sure you don't like a whole lot: 'Up against the wall, motherfucker, this is a stick-up.'" (As Todd Gitlin has noted, Rudd's disregard for Establishment institutions didn't extend to flouting the rules for using *whom*.)

As long as *asshole* could be outrageous and not merely coarse, it wasn't yet entirely naturalized as a Standard English word used by all groups and classes. But that process was already under way, even though the movement left and the counterculture had very little direct role in it. If you had to assign the emergence of the asshole to a period, it belonged to what the historian Bruce J. Schulman has called the "long seventies" that stretched from 1968 to 1984—though it would be just as informative to say it roughly coincided with the TV runs of *MASH* (1972–1983) and *All in the Family* (1971–1979). The tendency to associate the sixties and seventies with their most flamboyant and vociferous actors obscures the fact that, like all decades, these were lived out in a lot of places at once.

By the early seventies, it wasn't just the hippies who were letting it all hang out. The new frankness was also transforming mainstream mores and institutions. It was the age of *Playboy* and *Cosmopolitan*, of soft- and hardcore blockbusters like *Emmanuelle* and *Deep Throat*, of full frontal nudity and free-speech absolutism. Authors who had once used better words now only used four-letter words, as Cole Porter had observed thirty years earlier, though by now "four-letter word" denoted the ones beginning with *f* and *s,* not *h* and *d*. (Bemused by the new openness, the slang lexicographer Paul Dickson asked, "Is it my imagination or is there a law that requires all movies made after 1965 to have the word 'asshole' in them?")

Even lexicographers were swept up in the changing Zeitgeist; when the *American Heritage Dictionary* first appeared in 1969 it was the first major dictionary to include *fuck* and *cunt*—and not, it's safe to assume, owing to the influence of Jerry Rubin.

The pervasive cultural theme of the period was the informalization of social relations, one of those recurrent relaxations of ritual and manners like those of the 1920s, the fin de siècle and the Jacksonian era. The formal indicators of hierarchy and status were abandoned in favor of a conspicuous egalitarianism of address and interaction (in a 1980 piece in *Time*, Roger Rosenblatt listed first among the contemporary "voices of terror" the sentence "Hi. My name is Jeff, and I'm your waiter"). The new ethos was signaled by the mainstreaming of the counterculture's music, dress, and language, divested of any of the subversive implications they had acquired in the mid-1960s. The change in attitudes towards long hair on men was indicative. When the Beatles first appeared with their mop-tops, the style was ridiculed as androgynous but wasn't seen as a frontal assault on civilization. Within just a few years, though, long hair and beards on men were linked to "a wholesale attack on . . . the American way of life," as the *Wall Street Journal* put it in a 1968 editorial, warning that the counterculture's slovenliness signified "an assault not only on a political system but on the dignity of the individual and of human life itself." But by the 1970s, long hair on men had been thoroughly domesticated. The shaggy haircuts of the boys in high-school yearbook photos signified little more than what the anthropologist Edward Sapir once called "custom in the guise of departure from custom," as did the more coiffed versions sported by middle-aged businessmen. Jeans became a universal signifier of freedom, informality, and classless democracy—or at least until the end of the decade, when Ralph Lauren and Calvin Klein restored the old order of fashion. And the use of vulgarity, too, became a conventional badge of liberation from the tired strictures of conventionality.

Those shifts in lifestyle—itself a word that first became popular around 1970—facilitated the spread of *asshole*. More people felt comfortable speaking the word, and fewer were uncomfortable about hearing it.★ The word was becoming naturalized, even as the figure of the asshole came to populate everyday life. One way to think of this shift is to ask when and how *asshole* ceased to be slang. True, a lot of people still think of it that way—most dictionaries label the word as "vulgar slang." But to call a word slang isn't simply to say that it's highly colloquial or informal or that it's particularly vivid or colorful. Slang is in its nature an alternative language, "something that is willfully substituted for the first word that will present itself," as the great linguist Otto Jespersen defined it in 1922. By that definition, *short*, *wheels*, and *ride* are all slang for *automobile; bug off* and *scram* are slang for *go away;* and *chuck* and *deep-six* are slang for *discard*. But for us today, *asshole* isn't a colorful substitute for *jerk* or *boor*. It's the first word that comes

---

★The increasing frequency in print of both the anatomical and figurative uses of *asshole* over the second half of the twentieth century reflected in part the increasing willingness of publishers to print the word. But after 1970, the figurative use of the word increased far more rapidly than the anatomical use did, which indicates that this use of the word was independently becoming more popular. For more on this, see the note on the figures at the end of the book.

to mind when an asshole crosses our line of sight. *Asshole* has no prehistory for us: it doesn't seem curious or contingent that a single word should cover such a variety of offenders, and it doesn't occur to us that there might ever have been an alternative. The asshole seems as basic and universal a type of miscreant as the coward or the traitor. That's what it means for a concept to be naturalized: we call them assholes because that's what they are.

That process of adaptation happened remarkably quickly as social concepts go, but even so it could only take place by stages and degrees. Groups altered the word as they applied it to the situations and people that mattered to them, like an adolescent style that has to be taken in or let out a bit when it's picked up by the other gender or by a more mature market. And even as the word was spreading throughout the community, the very notion of authenticity that the word evoked was being redrawn in ways that touched every aspect of American culture, transforming the meaning of *asshole* along with it.

Country Boys and Cops

It didn't take long for the cultural and stylistic changes set in motion in the sixties to reach the white working class and make themselves known in the world of country music. At first there was resistance: in his 1969 "(Proud to be an) Okie from Muskogee," Merle Haggard had enumerated all the traits of the counterculture lifestyle that Middle Americans rejected, including marijuana, LSD, draft-card burning, beards and Roman sandals:

> We don't make a party out of lovin',
> We like holdin' hands and pitchin' woo.
> We don't let our hair grow long and shaggy
> Like the hippies out in San Francisco do.

"Okie" was generally interpreted as a panegyric to the "Silent Majority," a phrase popularized in a speech in that year by Richard Nixon, who proclaimed it one of his favorite songs and invited Haggard to perform it at the White House.★ Things had changed considerably by the time Charlie Daniels recorded "Long-Haired Country Boy" six years later. Long hair had become a badge of obstreperous redneck pride, and the range of consciousness-raising substances had been extended beyond white lightning:

> I don't want much of nothin' at all,
> But I will take another toke. . . .
> If you don't like the way I'm livin',
> You just leave this long-haired country boy alone.

★"Okie from Muskogee" was covered by performers ranging from George Jones to Devo to the Grateful Dead. There were several parodies, including one by the cult country singer Nick "Chinga" Chavin called "Asshole from El Paso": "We don't wipe our asses on Old Glory, / God and Lone Star beer are things we trust. / We keep our women virgins till they're married. / So hosin' sheep is good enough for us"—a reminder that *asshole* could be turned against the hypocrisy of cultural conservatives.

The spirit of Daniels' song was actually not that different from Haggard's. Both were defiant affirmations of proud independence and were solidly in the country music tradition of rebellious populism. In fact Daniels' political views were as insistently patriotic as Haggard's. But the style, trappings, and particularly the language had changed. Country outlaws like Willie Nelson, Waylon Jennings, and David Allan Coe wore beards and earrings and took advantage of the altered Zeitgeist to lace their performances with vulgarities, *asshole* prominent among them. The word had been a fixture of working-class speech since the war. Now it was made an emblem of contempt for the presumption and self-importance of middle-class professionals, managers, and other authority figures, a meaning that reclothed its World War II use in jeans and cowboy boots. The attitude was provided with an anthem in the early 1980s in August Campbell's "Asshole Song" ("The I-95 Song"), which was covered by numerous other country singers:

Were you born an asshole?
Or did you work at it your whole life?
Either way it worked out fine
'cause you're an asshole tonight.*

---

*Not to be confused with another "Asshole Song" written in 1993 by Denis Leary, who is also known for an abrasive working-class style:

I'm your average white suburbanite slob . . .
But sometimes . . .
I gotta go out and have fun at someone else's expense
I drive really slow in the ultra fast lane
While people behind me are going insane
I'm an asshole (he's an asshole, such an asshole)

It was around this time that law enforcement officers incorporated a similar use of *asshole* into their jargon. Recalling his days as a young San Diego patrolman in the late 1960s and 1970s, the former Seattle police chief Norm Stamper explains how the police divided the world into three categories:

> We dealt in pukes and assholes in those days. A puke was a longhaired youth who flipped you off, called you a pig, or simply had that "anti-establishment" look about him. An asshole, on the other hand, was a doctor, a lawyer, or a clean-cut blue-collar worker who gave you lip as you wrote him a ticket . . . The world was conveniently divided into "good people" vs. pukes and assholes.

And writing in 1978 about his work with police officers, the MIT ethnographer John van Maanen described a similar triage of the people officers had to deal with. He reported an apocryphal exchange that dramatized their notion of the asshole:

> Policeman to motorist stopped for speeding: May I see your driver's license, please?
> Motorist: Why the hell are you picking on me and not somewhere else looking for real criminals?
> Policeman: 'Cause you're an asshole, that's why—but I didn't know that until you opened your mouth.

From the officer's point of view, the asshole is someone who doesn't understand that whatever his social role or status, he's obliged to defer respectfully to the officer's authority and control. If he doesn't, the officer feels entitled to treat him abusively, to cook up an excuse to arrest or ticket him, or to subject him to "thumping" or some other form of street justice; as van Maanen explains, "the uncooperative and surly motorist finds his sobriety rudely questioned, or the smug and haughty college student discovers himself stretched over the hood of a patrol car and the target of a mortifying and brusque body search."

The officers' "asshole" category is a reaction to what Richard Sennett and Jonathon Cobb called the hidden injuries of class. It's a handy ersatz for the groups that impose cumulative indignities on them, like community elites, courts, politicians, and the press, whom the officers will never be able to confront directly. The label legitimates an aggressive response as an outlet for the officer's anger and frustration with both the individual asshole and the elite he stands in for. No less important, it creates a solidarity of shared values and experience among patrolmen, and not simply by drawing the members of the group together the way a common enemy always does; it can also "define to a surprising degree what the police are about."

That's a crucial function of *asshole*. Like any word that names a form of social deviance, it implicitly defines a social norm, as well. When we call somebody an asshole we make a claim about ourselves, not just individually, but collectively. "You're an asshole" implies not just "You're not like us," but also "We're not like you," and in an important codicil, "And we're like each other." As van Maanen says, *asshole* "swallows up and hides whatever differences exist among patrolmen." Often, indeed, to say we're not assholes is more specific than any positive statement we could make about ourselves. Like most derogative words, *asshole* lacks a positive antonym—what's the opposite of a schmuck, a nerd, a ditz, a phony, a scumbag? Vices are always more vivid and specific than the virtues they depart from.

The Rise of the Anti-Asshole

While it was hard to describe in precise words the asshole's antithesis, he could be personified in the figure of a new culture hero, the anti-asshole—or rather a set of culture heroes, one for each type of asshole that people discern. The police officers' asshole became the foil for the anti-asshole epitomized by Clint Eastwood's Dirty Harry, the model for the stock character who would be played in later movies by the likes of Bruce Willis, Steven Seagal, and Mel Gibson. Eastwood's Harry Callahan is tough, blunt, and disaffected. He is yes-ma'am courteous to law-abiding ordinary folk, but abusive and contemptuous to the criminals and lowlifes he has to deal with, and openly scornful of the people who keep him from doing his job: the police hierarchy, civilian authorities, the courts, the press, and other various other bleeding-hearts. Those antagonists are all assholes, a term Harry uses both for the bad guys and for his superiors. Told by his captain in *The Enforcer* that he is being transferred to personnel, he says, "Personnel? That's for assholes!" The captain stands up and says, "I was in Personnel for ten years" and Callahan responds, sardonically but sotto voce, "Yeah."

Like all archetypes, the Dirty Harry character has antecedents—you can see traces of him in the movies of Bogart, of Kurosawa, and of course of John Wayne. Wayne said in an interview that he had been offered the Dirty Harry role but turned it down, though after he saw the picture, "I realized that Harry was the kind of part I'd played often enough; a guy who lives within the law but breaks the rules when he really has to save others."★ But Harry operates in a different moral world from that of Wayne's characters. It's hard to imagine the laconic Wayne playing someone as volubly and obscenely sadistic as Dirty Harry is ("Fuck with me, buddy, I'll kick your ass so hard you'll have to unbutton your collar to shit"). Nor can we imagine any Wayne character giving free rein to Harry's ruthlessness and casual violence—choking a prostitute to get information from her, forcing a hood's head into a toilet bowl with a plunger and then flushing, blowing up a militant with an anti-tank rocket—much less admitting to taking pleasure in being given the excuse for it, as Harry does with his signature "Go ahead, make my day." And while Wayne could be insubordinate to his by-the-book superiors, he wasn't capable of Callahan's vulgar insolence:

HARRY CALLAHAN: Here's a seven-point suppository, Captain.
CAPTAIN MCKAY: What did you say?
HARRY CALLAHAN: I said stick it in your ass.

★Another story has it that Wayne was considered for the Dirty Harry role but was passed over. In *John Wayne: The Man Behind the Myth*, Michael Munn reports that *Dirty Harry*'s director, Don Siegel, said, "Wayne couldn't have played Harry. He was too old. And he would have objected to many of the things that Clint would do." A few years later Wayne starred in the unsuccessful *Dirty Harry* imitation *McQ*.

The difference, in short, is that Dirty Harry—and here I mean the archetype, not just the Eastwood character—is himself a kind of asshole. If we don't react to him as to an ordinary asshole, it's because everything in these films is contrived to make him seem righteous and his adversaries despicable. His superiors think only of their public image and keeping their jobs; the police psychologist spouts psychobabble; the minority leaders and the press are cynical and exploitative; and the arch villains are histrionically sociopathic—and usually middle-class whites who whine about their rights when they're finally disarmed. As a result, the viewer can enjoy the cathartic satisfaction of watching someone do and say really terrible things to people who manifestly have it coming. An unused studio tag line for the first Dirty Harry movie made the point unequivocally: "Dirty Harry and the homicidal maniac: Harry's the one with a badge."

The only thing that distinguishes Dirty Harry from the assholes he takes on—the thing that generally makes the anti-asshole different from the asshole simple—is that he knows he's being an asshole, a role he justifies in the name of moral duty. If there's some self-deception in that, Harry doesn't tip his hand—he never seems to worry about what it actually takes to make his day—which is what makes him at once a powerful cultural archetype and an artistic nullity. In other, more textured films in this genre, directors have explored the moral ambiguities of a hero's assholism to dramatic advantage. In the *Lethal Weapon* movies directed by Richard Donner, Mel Gibson's Riggs is unbalanced and suicidal, given to psychotic rages and even scarier simulations of them:

DRUG DEALER: Fuck you, man. That badge ain't real . . .
DRUG DEALER TWO: But you're sure as hell one crazy
    fuck!

Riggs' eyes begin to blaze. His nostrils flare. Like a maniac, he lunges at Drug Dealer Two.

RIGGS: You callin' me crazy!? You think I'm crazy! You, wanna see crazy? I'll show you crazy! This is crazy!

Riggs then proceeds to slap and pummel the Drug Dealer in the manner of the Three Stooges . . . complete with "WOO-WOO" sound effects. But he ends the routine by pulling a nine-millimeter Beretta from behind his back and pressing it against the neck of Drug Dealer Two.

RIGGS: That's a real badge. I'm a real cop. And this is a
    real gun.

There are even darker complexities in Detective Vic Mackey in the FX series *The Shield*, who is capable of killing an officer sent to spy on him, planting drugs on suspects, and letting a dog maul a cornered rapist. And then there's Detective Jimmy McNulty in David Simon's *The Wire* on HBO, a devoted cop, but one whose drinking, compulsive philandering, and self-centeredness exhibit an assholism that is evident to everyone: his superior ("You are a gaping asshole"), his ex-partner ("You're not the run-of-the-mill asshole, Jimmy, you're a special asshole"), the deputy chief ("the most swollen asshole in American law enforcement"), his colleague ("Natural po-lice. But, Christ, what an asshole!"), and his ex-wife and girl-friends. What redeems McNulty, at least in part, is that he defies the indifference, self-dealing, and other varieties of assholism that infest the apparatus of law enforcement and magnify the urban putrefaction at the center of the drama. The moral of the series is really not different from that of the Dirty Harry movies, though it's made deeper and more problematic. You have to set an asshole to catch an asshole, it says—ultimately, the same principle that drives the pervasive anti-assholism of public life.

The Real Stuff

For Harry, as for police officers and country singers, the notion of the asshole was rooted in a transformed notion of class. That's one thing that makes the asshole a creature of his age. There have always been disparaging terms for most of the people we think of as assholes, but almost all of them suggested someone of an inferior social class. Some were derived from words for bumpkins or laborers, such as *boor, lout, scut, knave, wretch, churl,* and *blackguard* (originally a menial who cleaned the pots and pans). A cad was a townsman who helped university students with odd jobs (the word is connected to *caddie*). Other words suggested people who gave themselves airs above their station, like *whelp, puppy,* or *upstart*. A *bounder* was, as one Victorian defined it, "a swell, a stylish fellow, but of a very vulgar type," someone beyond the pale of society, "out of bounds." In one way or another, that is, the words all leveled their criticism from above; they suggested someone who fell short of being a gentleman, either in his social rank or his character.

But *asshole* launches its attack from ground level, in the name of ordinary Joes, people whose moral authority derives not from their rank or breeding but their authenticity, which is exactly the thing that the asshole lacks. Inauthenticity is implicit whenever we speak of a "sense of entitlement," another phrase that entered the American idiom around the time *asshole* did. (It isn't necessary to qualify "sense of entitlement" with "unwarranted"—the phrase itself implies that the entitlement isn't justified.) It's telling that the increasing use of *inauthenticity* and *sense of entitlement* both tracked the spread of *asshole* in the language, as Figure 4.1 makes clear.⋆

The connection is intrinsic to the idea of the asshole, who imagines that his role or status gives him privileges that aren't really his to claim: the motorist who thinks his importance gives him leave to give lip to a patrolman, the boss on *The Office* who takes his position as justifying his meddling in the personal lives of his employees. The asshole's obtuseness makes him incapable of separating his sense of who he is from what he does or what he has or what he knows, which is what it means to be inauthentic. When you hear somebody say indignantly, "Do you know who I am?" it's a fair bet that he doesn't, either.

The growth in popularity of *authenticity* and *inauthenticity* was linked to a subtle but important change in their meanings. The words first became voguish in the 1960s. Around

---

⋆This and the graphs following were derived from counts of the words' relative frequency from year to year in the Google Books collection. For more on this, see the note on the figures at the end of the book.

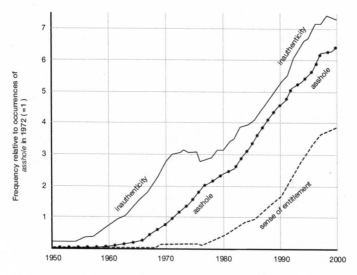

FIGURE 4-1. Assholes v. Inauthenticity v. Sense of
Entitlement

forty years ago, Lionel Trilling described *authentic* as "part of
the moral slang of our day"; you can only imagine what
Trilling would have made of books with titles like *Authentic
Personal Branding* and *Genuine Authentic: The Real Life of Ralph
Lauren*. If you listen only to the rhetoric of authenticity, very
little seems to have changed in the interval. Then as now,
people define authenticity simply as a matter of being oneself, doing one's own thing, knowing who one is; as one
book title has it, *Be Yourself, Everyone Else Is Already Taken:
Transform Your Life with the Power of Authenticity*. That leaves a
lot of room for variation, of course; "I Did It My Way" means
different things in the mouths of Frank Sinatra and Sid

Vicious.* But despite the rhetorical continuities, the notion of authenticity itself has been transformed, as well. As Abigail Cheever observes in *Real Phonies,* the postwar ideal of authenticity stressed separation and independence from the social context: "authenticity required defining oneself against the expectations of society and culture." To be authentic was to be a one-off—an iconic loner like Neal Cassady or James Dean, someone who's "not just one of the crowd," in the words of the Crystals' 1962 hit "He's a Rebel." By the end of the century, by contrast, authenticity had evolved into what Cheever calls "a standard of belonging," a way of affirming one's group identity. That isn't immediately evident from the things people say about authenticity—about being a maverick and refusing to kowtow to the dictates of fashionable views. Under closer examination, though, the brotherhood of the defiantly unfashionable swells to the 80-plus percent of Americans who define themselves as "politically incorrect," and the proof of one's authenticity is an association with a group that's viewed as unaffected and "natural," like the working class, blacks, or other ethnic minorities, or simply Middle Americans. It's not odd these days to hear politicians trumpeting their own authenticity, a claim that an earlier age would have considered self-cancelling. But when Michele Bachman, Rick Perry, and Rick Santorum say "I'm authentic," they're not evoking the shade of Neal Cassady.

---

*There are forty-three different songs at iTunes with the title "I Know Who I Am," variously classified as rock, hip-hop, jazz, Christian and gospel, alternative, R&B/soul, dance, and country.

They're pointing to credentials that make them just like everybody else—a childhood on a West Texas farm, a coal miner grandfather. (Iowa governor Tom Vilsack was admirably diffident about the claim when he was considering a run for the presidency in 2006: "I'm a Catholic from Iowa. My wife tells me I'm authentic.") And even if they haven't actually used the word, politicians like Sarah Palin, John Edwards, and Bill Clinton have staked their own claims to authenticity on the unprivileged backgrounds that give them a legitimate right to drop their *g*'s.★

But one can also assert one's authenticity indirectly, by identifying with the values of one of those *g*-dropping groups. That's the claim we make about obstacles when we call somebody an asshole; it presumes that we're authentic and that the target is on the other side of the line. Some of that follows from the word's vulgarity, in the modern sense of the term. To the Victorians, "vulgarity" suggested a connection to vulgar people—people who were, as the *OED* puts it, "coarsely commonplace; lacking in refinement or good taste; uncultured, ill-bred." Few people today would go near any of the terms in that definition: to describe someone as "common," "ill-bred," or "coarsely commonplace" sounds, well, vulgar. If there's still an idiomatic association between vulgar language and truck driver or "ghetto" speech, it's only by way of reinforcing the useful myths that give swearing its power—the

---

★Dropping your *g*'s is authentic but pronouncing them isn't, even if you were born to it. The only authentic accents are the ones we speak of people "lapsing into."

idea that vulgarity is an impulsive and unmediated effusion of honest emotion, unimpeded by middle-class affectation or delicacy. Those virtues are typified by the working class, whose members have ostensibly been spared the early repression that middle-class people are subjected to, but they're ones that any of us can achieve. From that point of view, class and status are like dealer options tacked on to the basic human being, and using vulgar words is evidence of an ability to set them aside and make contact with our immediate, authentic selves. When Dick Cheney was picked up by a CNN camera on the Senate floor telling Senator Pat Leahy to go fuck himself in 2005, the *Washington Post*'s Charles Krauthammer praised Cheney for his "demonstration of earthy authenticity" in a chamber in which authenticity of any kind is to be valued." The sense of "class" that *asshole* evokes, that is, is as much a matter of your attitudes and tastes as of your wealth or where you went to college. That's what enables Ann Coulter, out of Cornell by way of New Canaan, Connecticut, to effuse in a paean to New York City's outer boroughs: "Queens, baseball games—those are my people. American people."

It isn't surprising, then, that *asshole* entered the general American idiom around the same time that social groupings based on cultural values seemed to be superseding economic divisions, especially in political life. Thomas Frank tried to draw all of these factors together in *What's the Matter with Kansas?*:

> Class, conservatives insist, is not really about money or birth or even occupation. It is primarily a matter of authenticity,

that most valuable cultural commodity. Class is about what one drives and where one shops and how one prays, and only secondarily about the work one does or the income one makes. . . . In red land both workers and their bosses are supposed to be united in disgust with those affected college boys at the next table, prattling on about . . . big ideas for running things that they read in books.

This is a suggestive picture of the shifting conception of class in post-1960s America, and the last sentence in particular makes it very clear where the notion of the asshole fits into it: "those affected college boys at the next table"—what would you call them but assholes? Vague as they were, these class conceptions rested heavily on the identification of assholes, who could define authenticity by opposition, by embodying its antitheses. (As the pollster John Zogby has noted, summarizing the results of his surveys of American attitudes about authenticity: "Collectively, we Americans might not know exactly what 'authentic' is, but for the most part we know what it is not.") This is the moment that kicks off the assholization of American political discourse, when the qualifications for belonging to the "elite" shifted from power and wealth to lifestyle and attitude, blurring the word's political sense with the meaning it has in society pages and the names of florists.

No conservative has sketched this picture of class so fluently and plausibly as David Brooks, who also embraces the image of the country as cafeteria, but sees it as a less rancorous place than Frank does:

Americans do not see society as a layer cake, with the rich on top, the middle class beneath them and the working class and underclass at the bottom. They see society as a high school cafeteria, with their community at one table and other communities at other tables. They are pretty sure that their community is the nicest, and filled with the best people, and they have a vague pity for all those poor souls who live in New York City or California and have a lot of money but no true neighbors and no free time.

As recent events have demonstrated, both Frank and Brooks underestimated the extent to which antagonisms rooted in disparities of wealth are still simmering in the American forebrain. But that values-based conception of class is still a potent element, not just in political life, but in our everyday social thinking. Frank is right to assume that it emerged in its present form in the late sixties and seventies. But it wasn't initially the creation of the conservatives who made opportunistic hay of it. It was rooted in the same cultural shifts that reconfigured class distinctions in terms of consumer-based categories like *lifestyle*, *upscale*, *preppie*, and *yuppie*. As it happens, the frequency of those words increased in lockstep with *asshole* over the following decades, as Figure 4.2 makes clear.

This is as it should be. The yuppie was merely a specific form of the asshole: a self-absorbed, superficial creature of fashion, "generally out of touch with, and indeed antithetical to, most of the challenges and concerns of a far less well-off and more parochial Middle America," as one conservative

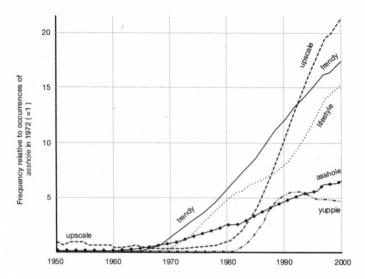

FIGURE 4-2. Lifestyle v. Trendy v. Assholes v. Upscale v. Yuppie

writer put it, in a reprise of Brooks' high-school cafeteria conception of class. (A popular joke made the connection explicit: "Why is a BMW like a hemorrhoid?" "Sooner or later every asshole gets one.") And since the yuppie category is defined by attitudes and lifestyle, it's one you can opt into or out of. You hear the word pronounced with unbridled scorn by people who would qualify for the label by any objective criteria, but who consider themselves exempted by virtue of their exemplary preferences in beverages and automobiles. Indeed, nobody pronounces the word other than scornfully. That's another thing that *yuppie* and *asshole* have in common: nobody thinks he belongs to either category.

Everybody's Word for It

Those revised notions of class and authenticity set the stage for *asshole* to become a fixture of middle-class conversation.★ By the early 1970s, the word was Standard English: virtually everybody knew it and owned the concept it denoted, even if not everybody was willing to say it aloud. That doesn't mean, of course, that the word is acceptable in all contexts, but then neither are many other eminently Standard English words like *hey*. But by this time it could appear in the mouths of middle-class characters in the plays and fiction of writers such as John Guare, David Rabe, Terrence McNally, and Neil Simon. Stephen King had middle-class high-school students using the word in *Carrie* in 1974, and Lanford Wilson put it in the mouth of a middle-class lawyer in his 1970 play, *Serenading Louie*:

> Alex: I read a report from the good old government that said we (meaning man) have discovered (meaning America, probably) just about all there is to know ... How would that asshole address himself to the complexity of the human being?

In no sense are these characters like the 1920s mucker-posers, who were trying to "emulate the language and manners of the bargee and the longshoreman," as James Truslow Adams

---

★*Asshole* plays a less prominent role in vernacular Black English than in Standard English. The linguist Arthur Spears doesn't discuss the word in his work on the use of obscenity in Black English, though he devotes a lot of space to other words involving *ass*. But he tells me that the role of *asshole* is often filled by *fool*.

described them. They aren't trying to sound street. The asshole has become a category in their personal moral inventory, linked to their sense of their own authenticity and humanity.

For middle-class speakers, as for others, *asshole* could sometimes be just a nondescript term of abuse. In a 1976 sketch called "The Street Fighters," Tom Wolfe noted the popularity of *asshole* in Manhattan's upmarket vernacular: "Asshole is the going insult this year. Everybody's an asshole. Immediately! Without a moment's notice! Never mind the preliminaries." Wolfe goes on to describe a battle over a cab between two homburg-hatted "Wall Street studs" clutching attaché cases:

> One has his hand on the handle. The other one bellies in. It's fierce.
>
> "Listen!" the other one says, "I hailed this cab!"
>
> "Hey! Watch it! I got here first!"
>
> "Ohhhhhhh, no! . . . Take your hand off that door, you asshole."
>
> "Who are you calling an asshole?"
>
> "You, you little asshole!"
>
> "Whuhh—I'll show you who's an asshole, asshole!"
>
> "Asshole!"
>
> "Asshole!"
>
> "Asshole!"
>
> "Asshole!"
>
> It's a chorus! A reprise! An opera! A regular Asshole Rigoletto.

Asshole doesn't seem to mean much more here than "fuck yourself." And it probably didn't convey a great deal more than that for Richard Nixon, who used it the Watergate tapes to refer to among others G. Gordon Liddy, Kwame Nkrumah of Ghana, and the Canadian premier Pierre Trudeau ("I've been called worse things by better people," Trudeau commented). The epithet wasn't wholly devoid of meaning—it probably reflected Nixon's insecurities about class—but it wouldn't reward one to linger over the subtleties. For the most part, though, the middle class was using the word as everybody was, to take down someone who seems to be abusing his status or claiming unwarranted privileges.

But middle-class speakers also extended the word to more refined strains of obnoxiousness, like the pretensions and preciosities of academics, artists, and intellectuals. For a typical example, take the way Martin Gottfried used the word to describe certain New York drama critics in a 1973 article in *Theater* magazine:

> Criticism of personal insult and abuse is not only irrelevant and sadistic but is usually witless and masturbatory. It is, in fact more difficult to be kind than cruel, as a simple matter of writing, and the very critics who style themselves acerbic— an asshole's style, if you ask me—tend when they like something, to be no fresher with compliment than with insult.

Snarky drama critics aren't a group that would have figured high on Dirty Harry's list of assholes. And as Gottfried's prose makes clear, he wasn't foregoing his own claim to membership in the literary *bon ton*. But there's a hint of intellectual Dirty Harryism in the obvious pleasure he took at calling the critics assholes, as a way of pulling moral rank to enlist the values of regular guys who aren't susceptible to the pretension or self-infatuation that licenses nastiness so long as it's put cleverly, even as he wasn't exactly bending over backwards to be kind himself.

The unrivalled master of this maneuver is Woody Allen. Allen's characters don't actually use the word *asshole* much, but the asshole type is a fixture in his movies, from *Annie Hall* to *Midnight in Paris*: the narcissistic intellectuals, manipulative New Age gurus and other assorted phonies who are served up as targets for ridicule by Allen or by one of his movie surrogates like Kenneth Branagh, Anthony Hopkins, Larry David, or Owen Wilson. All of these types show up in *Annie Hall* to be ridiculed by Allen's character Alvy. There's Annie's actor ex-boyfriend Jerry ("Acting is like an exploration of the soul . . . a kind of liberating consciousness," prompting Alvy to say, "I may throw up"). There's the memorable encounter with a man standing ahead of Alvy and Annie in a movie ticket line who's pontificating fatuously about Marshall McLuhan, until Alvy produces McLuhan himself from behind a poster to tell the loudmouth he doesn't know what he's talking about. And there's the clutch of academics at a West Side party that Alvy attends in flashback with his ex-wife:

ROBIN: There's Henry Drucker. He has a chair in
history at Princeton. Oh, the short man is Herschel
Kaminsky. He has a chair in philosophy at Cornell.
ALVY: Yeah, two more chairs and they got a dining-
room set.
ROBIN: Why are you so hostile?
ALVY: I wanna watch the Knicks on television.

Alvy slips off to watch the game in the bedroom, where his wife finds him and asks him what he finds so fascinating about a group of pituitary cases trying to stuff the ball through a hoop. "It's physical," he answers, "you know, it's one thing about intellectuals, they prove that you can be absolutely brilliant and have no idea what's going on." This is no less of a setup than in *Dirty Harry*—the odds of finding a roomful of West Side academics who are all indifferent to the score of the Knicks game are no better than those of finding a San Francisco police captain who would set a known serial killer loose on a legal technicality. But Allen's pseuds and show-offs are so airily pretentious and self-infatuated that they become easy foils for his derision, which might come off as obnoxious if its targets were drawn more three dimensionally. In his own way, Allen is as much an anti-asshole as Clint Eastwood—and the vicarious pleasure in watching him malign the assholes is equally satisfying.*

In one or another form, the asshole is a motor force in most of the movie comedy subgenres of this period. There's the smarmy or officious boss in office comedies like *Nine to Five* and later *Office Space* and *The Office*; the martinet teacher or administrator in *Animal House*, *Old School*, and *Fast Times at Ridgemont High*; the stuck-up frat boy in *Revenge of the Nerds* and, again, *Animal House*; the arrogant star athlete or

---

*In recent years, Allen's mastery of this maneuver has been rivaled by the postmodern anti-assholism of Larry David in *Curb Your Enthusiasm*. David never misses an opportunity to remonstrate indignantly with the assholes who plague daily life, like the "pig parker" who takes up two spaces or the "chat-and-cut" who strikes up a conversation with someone in line in order to slip in ahead of others.

coach of the opposing team in triumph-of-the-underdogs sports movies like *The Replacements*, *The Bad News Bears*, *Wildcats*, and *Major League*. Each type legitimates a corresponding anti-asshole, like John Belushi's Bluto Blutarsky in *Animal House*, Rodney Dangerfield in *Caddyshack* (tagged "The Snobs against the Slobs"), or Sean Penn's Spicoli in *Fast Times at Ridgemont High*—characters whose exaggerated grossness or disrespectfulness is justified by the humorless assholism of the comic villain. You think of Dangerfield in *Caddyshack* hitting the pompous judge played by Ted Knight in the rear with a golf ball ("a bum shot") and running his yacht into the judge's boat, or of John Belushi, in an unforgettable gross-out scene from *Animal House,* stuffing his mouth with a hard-boiled egg, then punching his cheeks together to spray it onto the fraternity and sorority jerks at the lunch table ("I'm a zit!"). Ultimately, the asshole receives his comeuppance when he's exposed to a public humiliation that makes his delusions and pretensions transparent even to himself. That was the repeated fate of Dabney Coleman, who made a career out of playing the self-important asshole in movies like *Tootsie*, *Modern Problems*, and most notably as the smarmy, exploitative boss in the office comedy *Nine to Five*—"a sexist, egotistical, lying, hypocritical bigot," as the Jane Fonda character calls him—who winds up trussed and swinging from the ceiling attached to a garage-door opener. (*Comeuppance* is a word made for assholes, with its suggestion of someone being brought face-to-face with his own vanity or presumption.) Or in a gothic version of the genre, the asshole is the jerk who's the first to get chopped up in a slasher film or the first to be chomped up in one of the Hannibal Lecter movies. But Lecter himself is the furthest thing in the world from an asshole. Whatever else he may be, he's scarcely self-deluded.

Insincerity and Inauthenticity

Nobody would be tempted to describe the humor of *Caddyshack* or *Animal House* as a comedic breakthrough. Humiliating the overbearing and self-important of the world has been a sure-fire comic staple from Aristophanes to the Marx Brothers. Yet something changes when the pseuds and snobs are reclassified as assholes. Their behavior may not be greatly different, but the rediagnosis casts it in a different light.

A generation earlier, many of those foils would have been called phonies, at the time a ubiquitous epithet for people who manufactured their public selves—people who "appeared cynically to conform to codes of behavior for social approbation or advancement," as Abigail Cheever puts it in *Real Phonies*. The obsession was given its definitive expression in *The Catcher in the Rye*. Holden Caulfield's world bristles with phoniness, which could come in the form of insincerity, snobbery, callousness, or calculated self-promotion. He discerns it in his teachers, in the fake-humble bow of the black piano player in a Greenwich Village club frequented by preppies, in the hammy acting of the Lunts, and in prep-school ministers (". . . they have these Holy Joe voices . . . I don't see why the hell they can't talk in their natural voice. They sound so phony when they talk"). He hears it in the conversation between his girlfriend Sally and a friend she encounters at the theater intermission:

It was the phoniest conversation you ever heard in your life. They both kept thinking of places as fast as they could, then they'd think of somebody that lived there and mention their name. I was all set to puke when it was time to go sit down again. I really was.

In his revulsion for phonies, Holden was speaking both for and to the fifties generation. *Phony* was the standard rebuke for the postwar preoccupation with appearance and status, the culture of William H. Whyte's *The Organization Man,* at the moment when *status symbol* and *status seeker* made their appearance in the language. It gave voice to a current of truculent individualism which was never far from the decade's superficial conformism, and which invigorated the Beats and other cultural rebels (the United States is "a rule of phonies," Allen Ginsberg wrote in his journal in 1960). A decade later those qualms evolved into the counterculture's rejection of the polluted, superficial mainstream, as "plastic" became an all-purpose epithet for the synthetic values of consumer culture that replaced authentic experience (as Frank Zappa put it: "I'm sure that love will never be a product of plasticity").

But denunciations of phonies and phoniness tailed off after 1970, at the same moment *asshole* was being incorporated into the American moral vocabulary, as Figure 4.3 shows. *Phony* persists, of course, as a label for an imposter, a fake (a phony ID) or a sham (a phony issue). And of course a lot of assholes have nothing to do with phoniness—that's the least of Donald Trump's issues—and not everyone who misrepresents himself is an asshole on that account. But as an indictment of character, phoniness is no longer the fixation it was in the

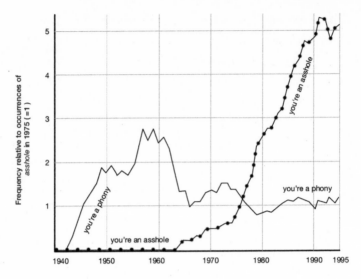

FIGURE 4-3. Phoniness v. Assholes

postwar decades, and the rise of the asshole clearly helped to nudge it aside.

The move from *phony* to *asshole* reflected a sharp shift in moral focus. Phoniness is strictly a matter of behavior. The charge has no particular psychological significance—phoniness can reflect cynical manipulativeness and self-infatuation, as it did for Holden's roommate Stradlater, or insecure defensiveness, as it did for Sally. Or sometimes it simply suggests the absence of an inner life, which is why the word is so often paired with *shallow* and *superficial*. Whereas calling someone an asshole suggests that his behavior comes from a distorted self-perception that feeds his obtuseness and sense of entitlement. That's why the asshole is not just contemptible but pathetic—not in the sense that he arouses our sympathy, but in the sense that he's ridiculous and miserably inadequate. (In Google Books, *pathetic* modifies *phony* just 11 times and *asshole* 147.) Recall Gregory Marmalard, the smug, handsome president of the Omega house in *Animal House*, sitting in his convertible with his girlfriend, unable to achieve an erection despite her perseverance ("Is anything happening yet? My arm's tired"). It's an affliction that's no more than his due as an asshole, but irrelevant to his being a phony.

chapter five

Men Are All Asshsoles

FERRIS: *Would you want to get married? I mean if I wasn't an asshole?*

—*Ferris Bueller's Day Off,* **1986**

"Men Are All Assholes"

The moral force of *asshole* rests on a connection between self-perception and social behavior, the idea that people who are deluded about their own importance are apt to be insensitive to the feelings and rights of others. Or to put it in other words, the asshole's sense of entitlement goes hand in hand with his lack of empathy. So it isn't surprising that *empathetic*, too, advanced in lockstep with *asshole* over the second half of the twentieth century, as Figure 5-1 shows.

It was that connection between entitlement and insensitivity that gave rise to a new use of *asshole*, as a label for men

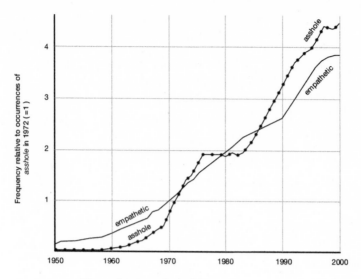

FIGURE 5-1. Empathetic v. Asshole

who behaved cluelessly or callously towards women. The new use of the word owed a lot to the rise of second-wave feminism, which had its cultural moment in the early seventies—the era of *Ms.* magazine and "I Am Woman," Judy Chicago and Germaine Greer, Billy Jean King and *Sisterhood Is Powerful*. It was then that "Men are all assholes" took wing as a stereotypical characterization of the program of feminism. Allusions to sexist assholes and chauvinist assholes became common, sometimes coming from feminists and sometimes from their derisive critics—the description of a feminist panel at the 1975 Modern Language Association meetings in *Change* began, "In the room the unattached women came and went and Michelangelo was an asshole."

But Jacobins and bluestockings weren't the only women

who were referring to men as assholes. Women were generally more comfortable using vulgar words by then, and not just among themselves. In 1971, *The Cosmo Girl's Guide to the New Etiquette* reassured its readers that "unless you have been wearing blinders and earmuffs for the last ten years, there is not likely a four-letter expletive a nice girl has never heard or even used."★ And women didn't require the urging of Kate Millett or Shulamith Firestone to see that a word aimed at people with an overinflated sense of entitlement might be a suitable label for men who were exploitative or high-handed in their relations with women. In a pivotal scene in the landmark cinema verité documentary *An American Family*, filmed in 1971 and shown on PBS two years later, Pat and Bill Loud are arguing in a crowded restaurant as their marriage is disintegrating. "I think that you're a goddamn asshole," she tells him—not something a woman would have said to her husband or lover a few years earlier, even in a John O'Hara novel. But by the 1970s the word was quite rapidly being adapted to the way men acted in relationships:

> What a pig! He must know that this has been an exhausting week and here he wants to come over and fuck me some more. What an insensitive asshole. (Nancy Weber, *Life Swap*, 1974)

★In fact women were evidently using *asshole* proportionately more than men were. A 1978 study of Massachusetts college students by Timothy Jay suggested that *asshole* made up a larger proportion of the taboo words used by women than of those used by men, whereas men were more likely to use *cocksucker, prick,* and, not surprisingly, *pussy*.

Elsa: You're really unbelievable, Will. You were an unbelievable kid and you ran away and saw the world and grew up and now you're back here. . . . what a stupid little asshole you turned out to be. (Israel Horovitz, *Hopscotch and the 75th,* 1974)

It was Amy's friend Cecilia, who'd had a terrific fight with her boyfriend and who was coming over to spend the night. . . . telling Amy she would never again see that no-good, low-down, you should pardon the expression, asshole again. (Lee Leonard, *I Miss You When You're Here*, 1976)

This was a powerful semantic maneuver. When you call a man who behaves callously towards women an asshole you accuse him of coming up short by the very standards that men themselves invoke to malign those who abuse their position in other ways—and in fact suggest that behaving that way is unmanly. I don't mean by that that *asshole* in general carries an implication of homosexuality, as some Queer theorists have suggested. There's no obvious homophobic cast to using the word of George C. Patton, Donald Trump, or an officious boss.★ But even so, using it of a man who behaves badly towards women is more or less literally a low blow: it makes him seem small and cruddy, and more than that, pathetic.

★But there's clearly a homoerotic undertone to *asshole buddy*, which emerged in World War II army slang about the same time that *asshole* did, though the phrase carried no explicit imputation of homosexuality. Its earliest definition, which appeared just after the war in *American Speech*, was simply "a comrade in arms."

Heel Replacement

Like other uses of *asshole*, this one involved a rediagnosis of an old condition and the dislocation of older terms. Before they were assholes, men who exploited women were variously scoundrels, bounders, rotters, cads, and more recently heels. Those words all faded with the rise of *asshole*, as you can see in Figure 5-2, which depicts the changing frequency of sentences of the form "He's a _____" in Google Books between 1910 and 2000. *Cad* was already on the way out early in the century, along with the Victorian notion of gentlemanliness that it was opposed to. But *heel* is a more recent word that belongs to popular American slang, and its gradual eclipse after World War II reflects modern changes in the way people think about relationships rather than about class.★ It was originally an underworld term for a rat or a double-crosser, but by the 1930s it was extended to a man who treated women cavalierly or heartlessly, exploiting them for sex or money. As Dinah Washington sang in 1946 in Jeanne Burns' "That's Why a Woman Loves a Heel":

> You know that he's a phony, more or less,
> But when he meets a lady in distress,
> He handles everything with such finesse,
> That's why a woman loves a heel!
> He knows just how to get beneath your skin,

★*Heel* is still used for the villains in pro wrestling, as opposed to the heroes, who are called "faces."

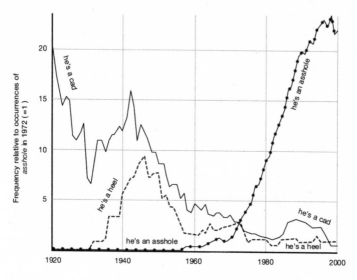

Figure 5-2. He's a Cad v. He's a Heel v. He's an Asshole

He holds the aces, you can't win!
He gets a lot of goodness out of sin,
That's why a woman loves a heel!

The forties and fifties were the halcyon age of literary and cinematic heels. John O'Hara's 1940 novel *Pal Joey,* about a nightclub MC who seduces a rich socialite into backing him in his own joint, became a musical play with Gene Kelly in 1940 and a movie with Frank Sinatra in 1957. There were Kirk Douglas as an unscrupulous producer in the 1952 *The Bad and the Beautiful,* Laurence Olivier as a womanizing music hall performer in John Osborne's 1952 *The Entertainer,* and at the end of the era, Paul Newman as a Texas rancher in the

1963 *Hud*, "insolent, appetite-ridden, but . . . terribly attractive" as the director Martin Ritt described him.

ALMA: Don't you ever ask?
HUD: The only question I ever ask any woman is "What time is your husband coming home?"

In a class of his own was the suave Zachary Scott, with his wavy hair and trim moustache, the arch-heel in *Ruthless*, *Her Kind of Man*, and most famously in Michael Curtiz's 1945 *Mildred Pierce*, in which Scott played the playboy Monte Beragon, who marries the self-made businesswoman Joan Crawford to keep himself in monogrammed shirts and then has an affair with her spoiled and selfish nineteen-year-old daughter, Veda. After Mildred discovers the affair, Veda tells her that she and Monte are in love and getting married, then later shoots Monte in a fit of rage after he disabuses her about his intentions with quintessential heelishness: "You don't really think I could be in love with a rotten little tramp like you, do you?"

Many of those characters would be described as assholes today, but *heel* and *asshole* depict their object very differently. Like the phony, the heel is seen only from the outside. He has no internal life that we care about and rarely gives any signs of conscience. He's indifferent to the pain he inflicts: he's simply "a cold blooded bastard," as Patricia Neal describes Paul Newman in *Hud*. Unlike the asshole, he's rarely described as insensitive—when you're dealing with a heel, questions of sensitivity simply don't come into the picture. Actually the heel doesn't miss much: "he knows just how to get beneath your skin," as Dinah Washington put it, which implies an acute sense of what's going on in a woman's mind. But that understanding doesn't lead to empathy, nor do we expect it to. The heel may or may not perceive what a woman is feeling, but he doesn't give a damn about it one way or the other.

The heel's stock in trade is to betray a woman's trust, by being unfaithful or by simulating affection for mercenary reasons. His sexual power puts women at his mercy even though they "know that he's a phony"—an effect that was definitively described by Lorenz Hart in the racy original lyrics to "Bewitched, Bothered, and Bewildered," which was written for the 1940 stage version of *Pal Joey* to be sung by Vera Simpson, the jaded wealthy socialite infatuated with the low-rent entertainer Joey Evans:

> Men are not a new sensation;
> I've done pretty well, I think.
> But his half-pint imitation
> Put me on the blink . . .

In the face of the heel's sexual allure, even a strong woman like Mildred Pierce or Vera Simpson is helpless. Those disparities in sexual power animated a whole constellation of dramatis personae in this period, such as the vamp or siren, the tramp, and particularly the sap, who was the heel's opposite and sometimes foil, as either the cuckold or the victim (I think of Edward G. Robinson in Fritz Lang's *Scarlet Street* as a uxorious husband brought to ruin by Joan Bennett and her heel boyfriend, Dan Duryea). Indeed, the disparities didn't always favor the man, though the victims of the heel and the vamp were depicted differently. The sap demonstrated an unmanly weakness in allowing himself to be manipulated by a woman's wiles, whereas the woman who yielded to the heel's attractions, while not exactly blameless, wasn't acting counter to her feminine nature—the sap had no female equivalent.

Men have never ceased doing the things that had earned them the label of heels, of course, but cultural depictions have changed. The noirish heel played by Zachary Scott or by Dan Duryea has been replaced by the slightly ridiculous ass-man of teen comedies, like Matt Damon in the 2004 *Eurotrip* or Ben Affleck as Shannon Hamilton in Kevin Smith's 1995 *Mall Rats*:

> SHANNON HAMILTON: You see, I like to pick up girls on
> the rebound from a disappointing relationship.
> They're much more in need of solace and they're
> fairly open to suggestion. And, I use that to fuck
> them someplace very uncomfortable.
> BRODIE: What, like the back of a Volkswagen?

And the rotter of sophisticated mid-century show tunes survives musically only in retro country songs like Carrie Underwood's "Cowboy Casanova":

> He's like a curse; he's like a drug,
> You get addicted to his love . . .
> He's a good time cowboy Casanova,
> Leaning up against the record machine.

That's a fine tribute to a bygone genre of heel songs like Porter Wagoner's 1967 "You Can't Make a Heel Toe the

Mark." But by now the notion of the heel is as outmoded as that of a Casanova, not to mention record machines. And the type can't be resuscitated, even in period dress. In the series' first season, *Mad Men*'s Don Draper treats women with the self-considering callousness that would have made him a classic heel if he appeared in a John O'Hara story. But the show's meticulous reconstructions of 1950's clothing and furniture can't evoke the attitudes of the era. Draper is no Pal Joey; the show gives us far too much of his anguished inner life to qualify him as a heel. In his relationships with women, he's just a twenty-first century asshole in narrow lapels and a skinny tie.

· · ·

Reclassifying the heel as an asshole imputes a psychology to him, a diagnosis of his condition. If the heel's offense is to exploit the natural ascendancy given to men, the asshole's offense is to delude himself that there is one—that the mere fact of being a man entitles him to privilege his own needs and appetites. At the same time, *asshole* implies a broader understanding of the man's responsibilities in a relationship. It isn't enough simply to be faithful or honest; the man has to understand and acknowledge the woman's feelings and the effects his actions have on them. In a scene from *The Wire*, Detective Jimmy McNulty has just had sex with Assistant DA Rhonda Pearlman. After they finish, she says to him, "You're an asshole, McNulty," and he responds with his signature line, "What the fuck did I do?" Actually, we're not exactly sure what he did, either. But whatever it was, it wouldn't have qualified him as a heel, but it does make him an asshole. What we have here is a failure of empathy: McNulty's cluelessness about his own conflicted feelings about Rhonda makes it impossible for him to understand, much less empathize, with her.

Or take a darkly funny scene in Woody Allen's *Deconstructing Harry.* Harry's wife, an analyst played by Kirstie Alley, has learned that he has been having an affair with one of her patients. In the midst of a session with another patient, she keeps interrupting her therapeutic conversation to leave the room and scream at him:

> MR. FARBER: I think I should quit my job, but I can't bring myself to do it. Maybe because my brother-in-law treats me kindly . . .
>
> JOAN: Er . . . excuse me one second (leaves him and we hear her off-screen while staying with Farber) . . . I can't believe you did this. You fucking asshole! . . . You fucked my patient! You don't fuck somebody's patient. That is a sacred trust!
>
> HARRY: What do you want? Who else do I meet? I'm working here. We never socialize.

By any traditional standard, Harry is a heel, "a double-talking, wise-cracking, tap-dancing liar," as one character puts it. But the film's focus is on Harry' inability to connect with his family or friends and his self-deluding rationalizations. He's no less contemptible than Zachary Scott, but he's more pathetic, and by the end of the movie even pitiable, unable to find anyone to accompany him to a university ceremony in his honor and brought face-to-face with his inability to function in life. (Google Books offers 147 hits for *pathetic asshole,* and just one for *pathetic heel.*)

Whatever the substantive achievements of second-wave feminism, it rapidly achieved a number of symbolic victories. Job titles were neutered, words like *coed* became scarce, and male executives became circumspect about referring to their female secretaries as "my girl." And for whatever reasons, men began to acknowledge the values implicit in the new sense of *asshole*, using the word to concede their blindness or insensitivity, usually after the fact:

> And then he stopped with the keys in his hand and he reached out for her very gently and held her close. "I'm sorry I've been such an asshole." (*Season of Passion*, Danielle Steele, 1979)

> "You're beautiful," he said. "What an asshole I was." (*Three Penny Lane*, Fielding Dawson, 1981)

In *Annie Hall*, too, Woody Allen implies that there may be a bit of the asshole in the way his alter-ego Alvy deals with women:

> ALVY: Well, I'm sorry, I've gotta see a picture exactly from the start to the finish, 'cause I'm anal.
> ANNIE: That's a polite word for what you are.

As Allen knows, saying that you've been an asshole in a relationship is one way of demonstrating the sensitivity that proves you're one no longer. Or sometimes, "I'm an asshole" can be offered as a variant of the it's-not-you-it's-me approach to facilitating a break-up:

Your eyes are all wet now,
You know that I'm lying,
I swear I was only protecting your heart.
But there are some reasons
And also some pictures,
Which if you saw they would rip you apart
And I won't watch you cry.
Goodbye, I'm an asshole.

—Jude, "The Asshole Song"

Men are more likely to confess to having been an asshole than having been a prick. You can recover from the first condition when you've seen the error of your ways, whereas the prick suffers from no delusion and hence has no error to perceive. There's a whole genre of films that turn on the personal redemption of an asshole, the modern reinterpretation of a plot line that stretches back to Jane Austen's Mr. Darcy. Tom Cruise has personified the type in a number of films: the self-involved, exploitative yuppie of *Rain Man* who finally abandons his plan to cadge part of the inheritance of his autistic brother; the self-involved, cocky pilot of *Top Gun* who has a change of heart when his aggressiveness causes the death of his radar officer; the self-involved, two-timing bartender of *Cocktail* who cleans up his act after the suicide of a friend; the self-involved, immature crane operator of *War of the Worlds*, the self-involved, misogynistic televangelist of *Magnolia*, and so on, each of them coming to appreciate the humanity of others after encountering his own frailty.

Backlashholes

To be sure, not all men who call themselves assholes are contrite about it, particularly in the era of the backlash against feminism and the reassertion of masculine prerogative. That's the attitude, in both senses of the word, that runs through reality TV shows like *Jersey Shore* and in the "you poke it you own it"–style beer commercials that show men behaving badly. (In an ad for Coors draft, a guy sets up a bar in his home, complete with a bartender, a pretty waitress, and a bouncer who refuses to let his girlfriend enter: "You're not on the list." "Bob has a list?" "Yeah, and you're not on it.") It's behind the emergence of what the *New Yorker*'s TV critic Emily Nussbaum calls the dirtbag sitcom—shows such as *It's Always Sunny in Philadelphia, Two and a Half Men,* and *Californication,* whose male protagonists are nonchalantly promiscuous. And it has given birth to a genre of lad-lit that has been called fratire. Some of these writers have tried to turn the asshole label into a badge of pride, with titles like *The Complete Asshole's Guide to Handling Chicks* and *Assholes Finish First,* Tucker Max's bestselling chronicle of his boozy sexual misadventures. At his website, Max explains:

> My name is Tucker Max, and I am an asshole. I get excessively drunk at inappropriate times, disregard social norms, indulge every whim, ignore the consequences of my actions, mock idiots and posers, sleep with more women than is safe or reasonable, and just generally act like a raging dickhead.

This posture clearly has some appeal for the sorts of young yobbos who walk around wearing "I'm an asshole, deal with it" T-shirts. But *asshole* isn't about to be rehabilitated as a positive term, no more than *bitch* is, outside of some feminist circles. In fact it really isn't meant as an effort at reclamation so much as a show of bad-boy naughtiness. There's a certain delusion in the assumption that there's some virtue in coming clean about one's assholism. The fact is that there's no such thing as an "honest asshole"; it's in the nature of being an asshole that you're obtuse about your entitlements and about the way others see you. If you're consciously and deliberately offending or manipulating someone, you necessarily belong to another breed. So when you hear somebody proudly declaring himself an asshole, it's a fair conclusion that he's not an asshole at all, he's just a dick.

But as we'll see, there's a current of another sort of assholism that runs through many of these backlash genres, particularly when they're justified in the name of political incorrectness. When a Yale fraternity has its pledges pose in front of the Yale Women's Center holding a sign that says "We Love Yale Sluts," the gesture means something more than guys leering at a sexy woman in a Super Bowl ad; it turns old-fashioned assholism into a political gesture.

The A-Word and the B-Word

In heterosexual relationships, the role of the asshole is reserved exclusively for the man, probably because men have always been thought of as singularly susceptible to the kind of insensitivity that E. M. Forster called the undeveloped heart, the failing of a long novelistic line of bluff, thoughtless males who say things like, "Good Lord, woman, now what's the matter?" It isn't a fair generalization, but it's one neither men nor women have had much of an interest in disputing.

But even leaving relationships aside, *asshole* is still applied vastly more frequently to men than to women. One big reason for that, to be sure, is that that's what most assholes are. The disparity is almost overdetermined. For one thing, there are simply more men in the positions of power that assholes are apt to abuse: if eight out ten bosses are men and 10 percent of all bosses are assholes, then 80 percent of asshole bosses are going to be men, independent of any gender differences in personality. Then, too, men are more likely to base their sense of self on their position or status, which swells their propensity to respond to challenges to their assertions of privilege with "Do you know who I am?" And men are more given to behaving officiously or aggressively than women are—more disposed to take a personal pleasure in bossing people around or in passing other drivers on the road and less willing to back down in the face of disagreement.

None of that entails that assholes are categorically male, but it does mean that men will make up a bigger slice of the asshole population. And to be sure, the word does show up alongside the names of women, particularly ones who are powerful or prominent, like Hillary Clinton, Lynne Cheney, Sarah Palin, Lady Gaga, Oprah Winfrey, and every one of the hosts on ABC's *The View*. But even when a woman does something that would manifestly qualify her as an asshole, she's more likely to be described as a bitch, so much so that people sometimes talk about *bitch* and *asshole* as if they were just names of the females and males of a single species, like *ewe* and *ram*. Yet the words are clearly different in meaning. *Bitch* is a much more general term—depending on the context, it can imply that a woman is lewd, unfaithful, frigid, malicious, treacherous, or imperious, among other things. Or often, *bitch* doesn't imply any specific fault at all, but merely serves as a misogynistic term of abuse that seizes on whatever unappealing trait comes to hand. (In the BYU Corpus of Historical English, the five most common modifiers of *bitch* over the past eighty years have been *little*, *old*, *stupid*, *black*, and *crazy*, with *white*, *fat*, *skinny*, and *ugly* not far down the list.) At a stretch, you could argue that there really is no such thing as a bitch, in the same sense that there's no such thing as a weed.★

Still, there are numerous traits which might lead someone to call a woman a bitch but which wouldn't make someone an asshole—being frigid, for example. ("She's a cold bitch" occurs more than two hundred times on Google, while "She's a cold asshole" occurs not at all.) Viciousness, too, is much more likely to evoke *bitch* than *asshole*, which doesn't convey the same sense of feral, hell-hath-no-fury rage. But there are cases where either word might in theory apply. Take the passenger berating the airport gate agent for not providing an upgrade. It's hard to see how the passenger's gender makes

---

★*Bitch* focuses on a woman as a social being, whereas the much more unspeakable *cunt* addresses her as a physical or sexual object. That's why *bitch* is more likely to be modified by words like *greedy*, *nasty*, *stuck-up*, *spiteful*, *vicious*, and *deceitful*, which imply intentional social actions.

any difference to the presumption or obnoxiousness of the act, but coming from a woman, the abuse is likely be seen as a violation not just of civility but of gender norms—"What an arrogant bitch!" Not that many people would say that the woman *isn't* being an asshole. But *bitch* is clearly the more demeaning insult, and the one that calls up a more visceral fear and anger. That's why people often use the word for women politicians they find detestable, on both the left and right. Often the word just suggests spitefulness or abrasiveness—"the crazy bitch from Minnesota"; "Who cares about this bitch from Alaska?"; "I see where the San Francisco bitch complained about O'Reilly." But it can also conjure up the specters of emasculation that in 2008 engendered the pants-suited Hillary Clinton nutcracker "with stainless steel thighs" (still available online at $24.95) and the spectacle of critics ostentatiously cupping their whizzers. As the MSNBC commentator Tucker Carlson put it, "Every time I hear Hillary Clinton speak, I involuntarily cross my legs."

Some feminists have urged that *bitch* be retired from the language; others have tried to repurpose the word, turning it into a reclaimed epithet like *queer*—a move that goes back to Jo Freeman's *Bitch Manifesto* of 1968 and the source of the names of numerous rock groups, songs, websites, and *bitch* magazine ("feminist response to popular culture"). But *bitch* works in that context precisely because it trades on the negative stereotypes it's associated with. The fact is that there are specifically female and male ways of being disagreeable and unkind, and there are times when it's convenient to have words for them, not least in the abstract (what would become of William James' "bitch-goddess success" in a neutered world?). That isn't to say that men can't be bitches or that women can't be pricks, but it requires some characterological cross-dressing.★ Still, as in other matters, it's a distraction to bring in gender when it isn't relevant to the point at hand. If Eddie Fisher was an asshole for dumping Debbie Reynolds for Elizabeth Taylor, then why wasn't Taylor an asshole for dumping Fisher for Richard Burton? If you think Barney Frank is being an asshole to the press, then why isn't Sarah Palin being an asshole when she does the same thing? It isn't just a matter of equity but economy of explanation. When both labels come to mind, *asshole* is always the more accurate and revealing judgment. If you can explain someone's behavior by pointing to a deluded sense of entitlement, why would you need to overlay it with a primordial female malignity? Assholes are assholes.

★It's true there's a long history of calling men bitches. Lighter describes this use of the word as "now rare except in homosexual use," but it was always a feature of Black English—it shows up in Ralph Ellison's *Invisible Man*—and has become more common in Standard English to describe straight men. Even so, my sense is that this use of the word very often retains some gendered associations ("Top ten signs he's a bitch. Orders a strawberry daiquiri on the first date").

chapter six

The Asshole in
the Mirror

There is nothing more theoretical than the language of the street.

—Paul de Man

Broken Hearts Are for Assholes

With its focus on inauthenticity, the rise of *asshole* seems of a piece with the familiar picture of the seventies as an age steeped in self-preoccupation—the period that Tom Wolfe called the "Me Decade," and that Christopher Lasch excoriated in his 1979 bestseller, *The Culture of Narcissism*. Those characterizations may be reductive, but clearly a lot of the energies unleashed in the sixties had clearly been redirected inwards. As Todd Gitlin recalls in *The Sixties*, his classic history of the movement left and the counterculture: "In the early Seventies it seemed that no ex-movement household was complete without meditations, tarot cards, group therapies, the Tao Te Ching, and the writings of Alan Watts on Zen, Fritz Perls on gestalt therapy, Wilhelm Reich on the recovery of the body, Idries Shah on Sufism . . . and most of all, Carlos Castaneda's parables of an intellectual's skeptical yieldings to the Yaqui Shaman Don Juan." The bookshelves of other households would have reflected a similar interest in self-discovery, though often along the less strenuous paths set out by best-sellers like *Jonathan Livingston Seagull*, *How to Be Your Own Best Friend*, *I'm OK, You're OK*, and Rod McKuen's *Listen to the Warm*. It's safe to say that there has never been an age that had so many buzzwords prefixed with *self-* (*esteem*, *-realization*, *-fulfillment*, *-actualization*, *-discovery*), or for that matter, that used the prefix so often its reproaches, as words like *self-absorbed* and *self-involved,* became dramatically more frequent. Whether or not the self was the only thing on people's minds, it was undeniably a major focus of interest.

For the middle class, that focus was nourished by an alphabet soup of therapies, cults, and movements promising self-realization and personal growth: Arica, bioenergetics, encounter sessions, Esalen, Gestalt, Insight Seminars, Neuro-Linguistic Programming, primal scream therapy, Scientology, Silva mind control, Transactional Analysis, and Transcendental Meditation, among numerous others. But the connection between assholes and inauthenticity was made most explicit in est, which was launched in 1971 by Werner Erhard, né Jack Rosenberg, a charismatic one-time car salesman who drew on the techniques of Scientology and Dale Carnegie. It became the self-realization program of the moment, endorsed by celebrities like John Denver and Jerry Rubin, and attracting several hundred thousand people to its seminars over the following decade. The program promised to "totally transform" participants by assaulting their belief systems until they "got it" (and if you had to ask what getting it meant, you hadn't). The transformations were accomplished in four-day workshops of fifteen-hour sessions during which the participants were seated on hard chairs, permitted few bathroom and meal breaks, and shouted at, lectured, humiliated, and submitted to interminable harangues in which *asshole* figured prominently as a term of abuse. The flavor of the sessions was reconstructed in *The Book of est*, a sympathetic account of the program by the est graduate George Cockroft, to which Erhard wrote the foreword. After the 250 or so participants have turned in their watches and agreed not to smoke, chew gum or leave their seats unless instructed to, a trainer addresses them:

MY NAME IS DON MALLORY. I AM YOUR TRAINER AND YOU ARE THE TRAINEES. I AM HERE BE-CAUSE MY LIFE WORKS AND YOU ARE HERE BE-CAUSE YOUR LIVES DON'T WORK. You are all—every one of you—very *reasonable* in the way you handle life, and your lives don't work. You're assholes. No more, no less. And a world of assholes doesn't work . . .

You're going to tell me all the rational reasons that what I say to you is stupid and I'm going to stand here and continue to call you an asshole and you are going to continue to be assholes. . . . It's not that you're weak or not trying hard enough. It's just that you're assholes, that's all . . . WIPE THAT STUPID SMILE OFF YOUR FACE YOU ASSHOLE!

Now the people who signed up for the est sessions were hardly assholes by ordinary standards—or at least not just for showing up; at the worst, that made them schmucks. They may have been conflicted about their "belief systems" and self-deluded about their identities; who isn't? But as most people understand the word, being an asshole isn't simply a question of being inauthentic but being perniciously so. Feeling like a victim or a fraud can be a way of making yourself unhappy, but if it doesn't lead you to hurt or disrespect someone else, you're off the moral hook—no harm, no foul. But as est used the word, *asshole* left one's effect on others out of the picture. If "getting it" meant accepting responsibility for oneself (even for one's hereditary diseases, as est told the story), it also meant release from fretfulness about whether one was doing the right thing. Even the effort to cease self-excusing and rationalizing was self-defeating; as Erhard put it, "An asshole is someone resisting being an asshole." If you felt guilty, ashamed, or remorseful, you hadn't gotten it. As Frank Zappa put it in a 1979 song, with maybe just a touch of irony, "You probably likes a lot of misery, but think a while and you will see / Broken hearts are for assholes."

In his 1978 book, *Growing (Up) at 37*, Jerry Rubin spoke of his involvement with est and the realization it brought him to: "Though I had rebelled against my parents, I had in fact reproduced their psychic structures within me." Addressing his parents, he said:

> You taught me to hate myself, to feel guilty, to drive myself crazy . . . I have your self-righteous right-wrong should–should-not programming . . . with that stupid JUDGE inside

me that I got from you . . . You taught me to compete and compare, to fear and outdo. I became a ferocious achievement-oriented, compulsive, obsessive, live-in-my-head asshole.

It was a confession of assholism typical of est, dwelling on Rubin's hang-ups rather than on the way he treated others. But for est, assholism was a purely solipsistic vice—you could be an asshole on a desert island.

Needless to say, the est trainers' liberal use of *asshole* turned them into rather monstrous assholes themselves—"monstrous" because unlike the anti-asshole personified by Dirty Harry or Bluto Blutarsky, whose asshole foils were real if overdrawn, the "assholes" that legitimated the abusive response of the est trainers were merely a factitious pretext for it. In a preemptive move, Erhard's acolytes half-acknowledged the point by calling themselves "estholes." But that term rapidly became a disparaging label for those who had undergone the process and insistently trumpeted its singular powers of transformation. As one disillusioned former follower put it, "Est turns introverted insecure people into extroverted insecure people." By the end of the decade, the movement had lost most of its cachet, dogged by charges of improprieties and charlatanism. ("There Is Nothing to Get," *Time* headed its article about the program.) The spectacle of people paying a couple of hundred dollars for the privilege of spending hours enduring a mix of vituperation and Kmart epistemology was irresistible to satirists, who made est risible in movies like *Semi-Tough*, *The Big Fix*, and *Bob & Carol & Ted & Alice*, not to mention a 1979 *Mork and Mindy* episode in which David Letterman played the mercenary founder of Ellsworth Revitalization

Konditioning, or erk (for network TV, "you're all assholes" was sanitized to "you're all dipsticks").

That was the fate of most of the more outré self-discovery programs of the seventies: either they were relegated to the cultural margins or absorbed in more low-impact versions in corporate training programs and motivational seminars. But the period left its mark on both the language and the ambient worldview. Much of the New Age language that Cyra McFadden satirized her 1977 bestseller, *The Serial*, is now unremarkable: nobody bats an eye at once-risible expressions like "I've got to get my act together," "I'm not into that," "It blew me away," and "Are you okay with that?" which inverted the psychological perspective of "Is that okay with you?"

Critics frequently depict those self-discovery movements and the rise of therapy in general to a culture of entitlement created in that period. In *How We Got Here*, his history of the 1970s, David Frum discerns the linguistic legacy of est whenever people tell a friend who has gotten into trouble, "I support you" or when we acknowledge a problem that has occurred on our watch with, "I take responsibility for that." According to Frum, the essence of est-speak is "its clever packaging of moral evasion as moral responsibility":

> What, after all, does it mean to "take responsibility"—as Attorney General Janet Reno ostensibly did after the conflagration of the Branch Davidian compound in Waco, Texas, that left eighty-six dead? She was not defending her action as right or proper under the circumstances but neither was she apologizing or expressing remorse . . . What she was saying, evidently, was that the action she took was taken by her.

These critiques of cultural effects of the era very often take off from Lasch's *Culture of Narcissism* or Phillip Rieff's 1965 book, *The Triumph of the Therapeutic*. Rieff's title is usually taken as implying that society is so absorbed with individual fulfillment that it crowds out concern for others. As one legal scholar has put it, "In the therapeutic culture, the self *is* the moral order." As the indictment goes, that view of moral values made itself known in, among other things, the culture of Oprah and Dr. Phil (whose book titled *Self Matters* seems to say it all), speech-codes aimed at protecting people against hurt feelings, an artistic aesthetic that prizes self-expression over significance, schools more concerned with instilling self-esteem than teaching math or English, the spectacular growth of what Ronald Dworkin calls "the caring industry," and a pervasive horror of making judgments of good and bad.

There's no question that these shifts in cultural attitudes had far-reaching consequences in law, education, health care, and business, for both better and worse. But the critique misses the real moral significance of the period's preoccupation with the self, in part because it draws too heavily on the public pronouncements of therapists, educators, and advocates. That makes for poor ethnography; when it comes to understanding everyday moral reasoning, it's a good idea not to believe everything you hear on Oprah. So it's worth coming back to the rise of *asshole*, the one cultural development of the period that we can feel confident wasn't motivated by anybody's higher ideals. There's no question that the adoption of the word reflected the period's psychological turn. As we saw, *asshole* is different from *heel* and *phony* in focusing on the perpetrator's self-deluded inner life rather than simply on his behavior. That's one reason why calling someone an asshole cuts both differently and deeper than those other words do: it's harder to live with being told you're pathetic and contemptible than with merely being told you're bad.

But being an asshole is anything but a purely psychological state. Jerry Rubin and the other votaries of est may have used the word for someone with an arrested self-realization, without reference to his behavior towards others. But *asshole* wasn't theirs to redefine. Then and now, when someone says, "I was an asshole," he's apologizing for what he did to someone else, not just for his own delusions or hang-ups. This is a far cry from believing that "the self *is* the moral order" or from defining away deviance as maladjustment or a social malady—"I'm depraved on account of I'm deprived," as one of the Jets explains to Officer Krupke in *West Side Story*. And it cuts much closer to the way people of that era actually talked and thought about their lives. The age that adopted *Asshole!* as its signature reproach for rudeness and insensitivity wasn't one that had bailed out on an external moral order.

Asshole and Narcissist, Separated at Birth?

The rise of *asshole* is the key to a much more general point about the period. The psychological preoccupations of the 1970s may have induced revisions in our moral vocabulary, but not in a way that cancelled or negated the moral significance of our actions. On the contrary, it was the vocabulary of psychology itself that underwent the most important transformation. Take the rise of the narcissist in the popular imag-

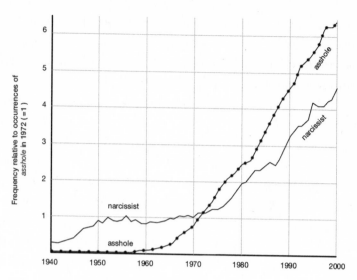

FIGURE 6-1. Asshole v. Narcissist

ination, which closely paralleled that of the asshole, as Figure 6-1 indicates.

The words draw their authority from opposite poles, of course, the one from clinical expertise, the other from the horse sense of ordinary folk. But they're the products of the same transformation of cultural attitudes and they serve many of the same purposes, even if they drive to work in different neighborhoods. Before the 1970s, *narcissism* was found only in psychoanalytic writing or Freudian criticism (which is what accounts for all of its usage before 1970 in Figure 6-1). Its entry into popular speech was mediated by self-help books and pop psychology, with a big boost from Lasch, who depicted modern culture as suffering from a pathological narcissism that made itself known in everything from the popularity of streaking and jogging to cults of "pseudo self-awareness" and a fascination with oral sex. By the 1980s *narcissist* was appearing in *Parents* magazine, stories about Joe Namath, and the astrology column of *Mademoiselle* ("Libra beauty profile: A bit of a narcissist, you love to be pampered, massaged, and manicured").

The rise of *narcissism* was one of the linguistic reflexes of Rieff's "triumph of the therapeutic," which contributed a spate of words to everyday speech—*alienation, conformist, identity crisis, antisocial, repressed hostility*, and *sibling rivalry*. At first glance, the process seems to mirror the medicalization of other social values, as the old, morally charged categories are replaced by scientific ones that suspend subjective judgment. When *drunk* gives way to *alcoholic*, we pass "from badness to sickness," in the words of the subtitle of a classic text on deviance (itself a word that became dramatically more frequent in the postwar period).

But the colloquialization of terms from clinical psychology didn't always signal the moral evisceration of the concepts they stood for. Words like *narcissism* aren't doing the same thing as *alcoholic* or *PTSD*. Rather, they're aimed at blurring the line between the psychological and the moral, so that a diagnosis of a mental disorder provides a proof of moral rot. When Bernard Madoff was exposed as a swindler, *Forbes'* Susan Lee contacted several psychoanalysts with reputations for being "extremely penetrating" to find out what made Madoff do it. She reported that "their diagnosis was immediate and unanimous: narcissistic personality disorder—someone who displays grandiosity, needs admiration and lacks empathy." Therapists consulted by other journalists explained Madoff's behavior as a symptom of psychopathy or addictive dysfunction. But whatever the diagnosis, it wasn't offered to mitigate Madoff's crimes, much less recommend a course of treatment. This wasn't an occasion for "depraved on account of he's deprived" extenuations or for speculating on what in Madoff's past might have brought about the disorder (an early narcissistic injury? schlocky genes?). The diagnoses were meant to establish that Madoff was officially and clinically aberrant, twisted, morally deformed. It was really just a matter of giving a medical stamp of approval to the judgment given by the actress Kyra Sedgwick, one of Madoff's victims: "He's a sick man."

In ordinary usage *narcissism* is mostly just "a loose synonym for bloated self-esteem," as Peter Gay described it in his biography of Freud. The list of commentators and columnists who have diagnosed the president as a narcissist ranges from George Will and Charles Krauthammer to Stanley Fish and Lyndon Larouche. The charge isn't different from the charges of self-importance that were leveled at Lincoln, Wilson, and FDR, though in Obama's case it can translate either as cocky, which is fair, or as uppity, which is a bit more problematic. But now it comes wearing a lab coat and accompanied by counts of first-person pronouns to invest it with a specious empirical sheen. Others have discerned the condition in Nancy Pelosi, Sarah Palin, and Newt Gingrich, to name a few, consulting the *Diagnostic and Statistical Manual of Mental Disorders* as if it were *Peterson's Birds of North America*. Some of those people may indeed manifest the symptoms of pathological narcissism as listed in the "any five of the following" definition in the *DSM* (or at least until the appearance of *DSM5*, which will eliminate any reference to the disorder)—

they're people who need admiration, are arrogant or haughty, have a sense of entitlement, and so on. But you could say all that about them in English.

In their social connotations, the distance between *narcissist* and *asshole* is vast. Semantically, though, they're close twins. When somebody is described as "a narcissistic asshole"—a phrase that gets thousands of hits on Google—the *narcissistic* isn't there to distinguish one type of asshole from another (as in ". . . as opposed to an obsessive compulsive one"). It's just an idiomatic intensifier like the adjectives in *blithering idiot* and *unmitigated gall*. For that matter, people sometimes talk about being an asshole as if that were a clinically defined disorder as well. According to an article in *Psychology Today* ("Do Girls Really Love Assholes?"):

> In terms of psychology, the "asshole" consists of the following traits: High Extraversion, Low Neuroticism (perhaps), Low Conscientiousness, Low Agreeableness, High Openness to Experience, and a bit of a dip into the dark triad traits (those with an extreme dark triad profile aren't considered sexually attractive). The dark triad refers to three personality deficiencies: narcissism, Machiavellianism, and psychopathy.

This feels like therapeutic overreach, as if assholism was just the vulgar name for some region in the map of personality disorders. But actually, it tells us less about *asshole* than it does about how therapeutic language has been co-opted to express our disgust and indignation. It isn't that *asshole* has become a synonym for *narcissist*, but that as most people use the word, *narcissist* has become a synonym for a certain kind of asshole.

What Makes Assholes Assholes?

The most striking thing about the pairing of *narcissist* and *asshole* may be the empty space that's left between them. Taken together, they signal the attenuation of the high moral language of public life. To express the full extent of your indignation over Madoff's crimes, you can go one of two ways: you can call him a sociopath or a narcissist, or you can call him a scumbag or a piece of shit. But you can't describe him as a scoundrel, as evil, or as a heartless wretch—or at least not without a theatricality that undercuts the genuineness of your feeling. *Scoundrel* is a fine-sounding word, but it isn't the one you'll choose to convey your genuine anger to a friend who has lost all her money in a swindle.* That tendency to replace a moral vocabulary with its roots in literature and criticism by one with roots in science is the most dramatic linguistic effect of Reiff's rise of the therapeutic. But what it shows is mostly how the moral mindset defeats any effort to keep it at a clinical distance. People always find a way to express their disapproval, whether the words they use are actually designed for that purpose.

Words like *narcissism* acquire their moral weight through a kind of semantic sleight of hand; we treat them as objective

---

*After Madoff was exposed, Elie Wiesel, whose Foundation for Humanity had lost a huge amount of money in the scam, said that *psychopath* was "too nice a word" for Madoff: "Sociopath, psychopath, it means there is a sickness, a pathology. This man knew what he was doing. I would simply call him thief, scoundrel, criminal." But Wiesel was expressing a somewhat Old World view: in modern American discourse; there's nothing "nice" about calling someone a sociopath.

scientific categories at the same time we deploy them as subjective judgments. A blog commenter put the point deftly in a discussion of malignant narcissism: "It may be a disease, but they're still assholes." But *asshole* belongs to us, not to the compilers of the *DSM*, and the link it draws between personality and character is an intrinsic part of its meaning. The asshole's delusion and inauthenticity is his own fault, not nature's. If it weren't, assholes wouldn't be assholes.

Take, once last time, Norman Mailer's Lieutenant Dove:

> Hearn remembered Dove's saying to him once when he first came to the division, "You know, really, Hearn, you can appreciate this because you're an educated man like me, but do you know there's sort of a coarser element in the officers in the Army? The Navy's more careful."

Why does Dove merit the label *asshole*? Sure, he's full of himself and thinks his social class makes him superior to the other officers. But his condescending airs don't actually injure anyone, and like a lot of phonies and poseurs he lacks what lawyers call *mens rea*, the intent to do harm. On the basis of what Mailer tells us about him, we wouldn't be tempted to call him a prick or a shit or a bastard.

But Dove is mortally obtuse, in the sense of the word that the *OED* defines as "annoyingly unperceptive; stupid; insensitive." "Annoyingly" is the key: obtuseness is a culpable failure to acknowledge what ought to be evident, particularly when it touches on the needs or interests of others. We don't use the word for someone who turns a blind eye to realities through inattention or wishful thinking, like the terminal cancer patient who refuses to face the hopelessness of his prognosis. Assholes like Dove are obtuse in two directions at once. Their self-infatuation leads them to repress inconvenient realities at the same time they imagine that those realities aren't obvious to anybody else, either. To use an expression that wouldn't enter the language until some time after the book was published, Dove thinks he's hot shit, and he's studiously oblivious to the fact that Lieutenant Hearn and the other officers don't agree—or indeed, that Hearn considers him a vulgarian. But then, Dove couldn't very well delude himself if he didn't also imagine he was fooling the others.

It's that obtuseness that leads one to ask, "Whatever could this person be thinking?" when considering the behavior of some exemplary asshole—not a question we're tempted to ask about somebody we've written off as a heel or a prick. Obtuseness requires a capacity to recognize and understand things—you can only be obtuse about something that ought to be obvious to anyone with your intelligence and experience. It's easy to think of small children as little shits, since a predisposition to malice or cruelty can manifest itself very early on. But we rarely describe little children as assholes. You can't be an asshole until you're old enough to know better, and neurotic enough to sense that you ought to feel bad about it. If we weren't vaguely aware of how unreasonable our presumptions were, we wouldn't need to conceal them from ourselves or cook up excuses for them. To call someone an asshole is to imply he has a conscience, which is why the term is really incompatible with clinical psychopathy—why no one would use it for Hannibal Lecter, say. And it's what leads us to think of assholes as unhappy people, whose delusions don't quite conceal from themselves their moral deformities. They don't know that they're assholes, at least at the moment, but they sit uncomfortably in their skins.

Obtuseness is the true measure of the asshole. We calibrate how much of a prick or bastard or fucker someone is by the amount of harm he's willing to inflict. But we reckon the degree of someone's assholeness not by the actual hurtfulness of his behavior but by the breadth of his self-delusion, the discrepancy between his perceptions and the reality before his eyes, the energy of his denials and rationalizations. The greater the gulf, the more of an asshole he is. We're much more likely to describe somebody as a blatant asshole than as a blatant prick or bastard—it's like talking about "blatant stupidity," where *blatant* refers to the obviousness of what the asshole is pretending not to see. Donald Trump, Gordon Ramsay, Gene Simmons, Charlie Sheen—titans of assholism, all of them, but not because of the actual evil they do. Those are the assholes we describe as "flaming" or "outrageous" for their ease in discounting the feelings of others and their seeming obliviousness to how they're coming off. And not incidentally, they've all done very well for themselves by it. If you have to be a flaming asshole, this is a good age to be born in.

chapter seven

The Allure of
Assholes

It is false, this teaching of decay.
—James McNeill Whistler

The Teaching of Decay

Ask people whether this is an age of assholes, and they'll very likely answer yes. Pollsters don't put the question in exactly those terms, of course, but surveys consistently find more than three-quarters of Americans saying that people are less respectful than they once were, that the level of civility is declining, and that drivers are less courteous, among other things.* And the idea of decline is implicit in the complaints

---

*In a 2002 Public Agenda poll, 73 percent of the respondents agreed that "Americans used to treat each other with more respect and courtesy," while only 21 percent said "this is just nostalgia." In a 2010 poll by KRC Research, 80 percent said the level of civility had gotten worse, and only 9 percent thought it had gotten better.

about endemic plagues of narcissism and entitlement that have become a compulsory floor exercise for op-ed opinionators.

But it isn't that simple. For one thing, the answer to the question "Have we gotten ruder?" has always been yes. Since the early Victorian era, there has never been a moment when critics weren't looking back wistfully on the decorum that prevailed a generation or two earlier. People have been bemoaning the disappearance of "old-fashioned courtesy" since Dickens' day—indeed, the term "old-fashioned" itself reflects the universal assumption that true manners are a bygone virtue. (In the twenty-five billion or so web pages indexed by Google, no one has so much as a word of praise for "the very latest courtesy" or "up-to-the-moment politeness.")

Yet the very persistence of those complaints seems to undermine them. As Montesquieu said, looking back across an unbroken line of lamentations about the decline of virtue that stretched back to Horace and Aristotle: "If this all were true, men would be bears today." As you take a longer historical view, the idea of decline seems increasingly implausible. Only someone with a defective literary education could maintain that there are more assholes in circulation now than there were cads, bounders, and blackguards running around in the age of Thackeray and Dickens, who hardly lacked for material in that line. And even looking just over the recent past, it isn't all bad news. We might give ourselves a little credit for how far we've come since the era depicted in *Mad Men* and *Revolutionary Road*, at least by our own lights, and for all the forms of rude and offensive behavior we've driven to the social margins. Think how many of the comments about race, gender, and sexual orientation public figures have been forced to apologize for in recent years that wouldn't have been considered gaffes if they had come to light a half century ago. It's up for grabs whether we've actually become more tolerant than we used to be; there are times when our embrace of the rhetoric of tolerance serves only to make our exercises of intolerance subtler and more oblique. But we do acknowledge tolerance as a virtue to which everyone is obliged to pay conspicuous tribute, and what does civility come down to in the end but making a show of consideration and good intentions? Civility is a matter of appearances, not motives—a manner, as Hume put it, whereby "a mutual deference is affected [and] contempt of others disguised."

Still, the sense of decline is hard to shake. Hume thought it was baked into us: "To declaim against present times, and magnify the virtue of remote ancestors," he wrote, "is a propensity almost inherent in human nature." Montesquieu himself suggested that it stemmed from the memory of the criticisms of our shortcomings that we endured from our parents and teachers, so that each generation feels itself unequal to the previous one. Or maybe the explanation is purely cognitive: we simply react more acutely to novel forms of discourtesy than to the ones we've gotten used to. That's no doubt why I find it more annoying to click on a link in an email that ostensibly comes from LinkedIn and find myself at the web page of a Canadian pharmacy than to open a letter that looks like an official notice and discover it's from a mortgage broker. It isn't as if the first is any harder to discard than the second, after all.

Here's another theory. In *On Rude Democracy*, Susan Herbst suggests that the perception of growing incivility reflects a heightened sensitivity to displays of rudeness: "The Oprah-like culture of therapy—feeling good about our human interactions, or at least not feeling bad—has led us to avoid, or at least be disturbed by, even minor feelings of discomfort in political discourse, whether televised, on the Web, or in person." On the face of things, this is a bit hard to square with the popularity of political talk shows and the other boisterous formats of public life. But something rather like it may explain the sense of panic about the forms of incivility that seem to pervade everyday life: the bullying, the screaming Little League coaches and parents, the road rage and air rage, the snippy salespeople and pissy customers, the abusive bosses and querulous employees.

The anecdotes and incidents can be chilling, but are any of these really a growing problem? There has been a spate of business books warning about the personal and economic costs of workplace incivility, but you could argue that rudeness has always been a feature of the workplace, and that the big difference is that now we're concerned about it. You could make that point about bullying, too. Despite the headlines, the indications are that bullies are no more of a problem than they used to be, and quite possibly less of one. According to the National Center for Educational Statistics, in 1995 12 percent of students reported "being afraid of attack or harm at school"; in 2009 the number had dropped to 4 percent. That doesn't mean bullying isn't deserving of our attention, all the more since technology provides new outlets for it. But the real change is in our decreasing tolerance for it, not its increasing prevalence. And so on for other indignities of daily life. The long history of discourteous driving is documented in the appearance of words from *road hogging* (1906) to *speed-ster* (1918) to *tailgating* (1951). And there's a line of complaints stretching back for more than a century about the ill-man-nered people one encounters in department stores: the cus-tomers who pushed you out of the way at the sales racks and forced their way into elevators, and the "rudeness, stupidity, and indifference" of the clerks that a writer in *Munsey's Mag-azine* deplored in 1900.

If you looked only at the history of those complaints, you could easily conclude that nothing had really changed since Montesquieu's time. But while grumbling about rude neigh-bors and mean bosses is an eternal diversion, that isn't really the kind of incivility that's behind the present sense of crisis. In surveys, people overwhelmingly say that incivility is not a major problem in their relations with co-workers or their friends or around the family dinner table. (Ironically, they also lay the blame for its rise on the failure of parents to instill a sense of proper behavior in their kids when by their own ac-counts the family is the one institution that seems to be doing its job here.*) The areas where people see civility breaking down tend to be ones that are remote from the face-to-face interactions of everyday life, like politics, the media, and the Internet. Those are the settings in which the most dramatic changes in behavior have taken place, and whether or not

---

*In a 2002 Public Agenda survey, 84 percent of respondents agreed that "too many parents are failing to teach respect to their kids." But in a more recent survey by a division of Interpublic, only 13 percent of respondents saw incivility as a problem among friends and family, and just 7 percent said it was a problem at the family dinner table. By contrast, politics was judged uncivil by 80 percent, closely fol-lowed by areas that include "pop culture," the media, and professional sports.

they're really a cause for alarm, they do raise unprecedented questions. This isn't an age of assholes—or at least there are no more of them walking the earth than there used to be back when they went by other designations. But it's fair to call it an age of assholism, one that has created a host of new occasions for acting like assholes and new ways of performing assholism, particularly among strangers and in public life.

· · ·

Technology has played a big role here, as it always has in the past. Since the nineteenth century, every new form of communication has multiplied the opportunities for unwelcomed intrusions on our persons and privacy. Henry James wrote of telegraphists who exploited the secrets they gleaned from their patrons' communications. The telephone made the home accessible to unsought intrusions from strangers and left daughters prey to the allurements of undesirable suitors: "The serenading troubadour can now thrum his throbbing guitar before the transmitter undisturbed by apprehensions of shotguns and bulldogs," one writer warned in 1884, adding that without an exchange of letters, there could be no grounds for a breach of promise action. Etiquette columnists of the 1950s took after people who blared their music in public over transistor radios. ("There's No Escape," *Life* magazine headed its article on the problem in 1961.) Nowadays the problem is the ones who retreat into a shell behind their earbuds or impose one-half of a cell phone conversation on bystanders.

In their power and ubiquity, digital technologies introduce hitherto unimaginable possibilities for being uncivil and inconsiderate: cyber-bullying, tweeting or checking your mail in the middle of a meeting, posting anonymous defamations about an ex-boss or ex-girlfriend, spamming the subscribers to a mailing list, lurking and trolling on blogs and discussion lists, and all the other forms of misbehavior that new media have given rise to. The very ease of the technology can exacerbate matters; Michael Kinsley suggests that "banging out an e-mail is just so easy, compared with all the necessary elements of writing a letter, that the id can send out a half-dozen e-mails before the superego can stop it." And it takes just a slip of the finger to broadcast an indiscretion to a vast audience: you write an email to a colleague describing someone as an asshole, mistakenly click on "reply to all" instead of just "reply," and bingo, it's on the screens of 260 other people on the recipient list.

Add to that the automation of the service economy, which seems designed to draw our inner asshole to the surface. If we find ourselves being a little more peckish than we used to be when we call the cable company with a question about our bill, it's because we've had to punch 4, then 3, then 1, then punch in our account number, and then wait on hold for ten minutes before being put through to an agent, who asks for our account number a second time and then has to patiently endure our remonstrances—it's a tough way to make a living, dealing with assholes like us all day. You could put a positive spin on this by saying that the modern world provides us with more opportunities to make a display of forbearance, but not many of us are up to thinking about it that way.

Three Assholes for the Age

But this is also an age of assholism simply because we find the phenomenon and its practitioners so interesting—or provocative, or compelling, or compellingly repulsive, or sometimes all of those at once. I'm not thinking so much of assholes of opportunity like Charlie Sheen and Mel Gibson, or of incidental assholes like James Cameron or Brett Favre, whose assholism only adds a colorful sidebar to an independently impressive career. There's little about those people that's particular to the age, save that in earlier periods the public probably would have been spared the details of the personal tics and twitches that qualify them for the asshole label. What's unique to our time is the fixation with certain iconic assholes, who exemplify each in his way the problematic allure of the species.

Steve Jobs, for example, was a modern personification of the asshole as achiever, someone whose assholism seems to be inextricable from his success as a leader. The traditional paragons of the type are the storied tough guys from military, business, and public life whose leadership styles are packaged in memoirs and advice books like *What It Takes to Be #1: Lombardi on Leadership,* Rudy Giuliani's *Leadership, 29 Leadership Secrets from Jack Welch*, and above all a four-foot shelf of inspirational works on George S. Patton, the first general to have been explicitly designated an asshole by both his men and his superiors. From *Patton on Leadership: Strategic Lessons for Corporate Warfare*, we learn:

If he slapped a soldier, well, it was certainly wrong, but he thought it necessary for the morale of his troops. . . . It was often said that his troops would accomplish the impossible, then go out and do it all over again. "Patton's men" may not have always truly appreciated the man's leadership style at the time. Human nature is such that the discipline and the obedience required by a great leader are so often cause for griping and displeasure. But in retrospect, to have served under Patton was a red badge of courage to be worn forever.

The passage is calculated to reassure even the most abusive manager that he's on the right track; it's for the good of the team, after all, and whatever his subordinates may say about him, they'll be grateful later on.

For some, Jobs fills an analogous role in the digital age. Shortly after his death and the publication of Walter Isaacson's bestselling biography, Tom McNichol wrote in the *Atlantic*:

CEOs, middle managers and wannabe masters of the universe are currently devouring the Steve Jobs biography and thinking to themselves: "See! Steve Jobs was an asshole and he was one of the most successful businessmen on the planet. Maybe if I become an even bigger asshole I'll be successful like Steve."

And indeed, some observers depicted Jobs' assholism as a deliberate management style. As Alan Deutschman put it in *Newsweek*, Jobs was a "master of psychological manipulation":

He found that by delivering brutal putdowns of his co-workers he could test the strength of their conviction in their own ideas. . . . He found that many of the most brilliant engineers and creative types actually responded well to cruel criticism, since it reinforced their own secret belief that they weren't living up to their vaunted potential.

Not everyone agrees with that assessment of Jobs' skills as a manager; Isaacson says that he was terrible at it, and that success came despite his being a colossal asshole, not because of it. But it isn't as if there are no advantages to being an asshole, in business or elsewhere. Life rarely makes moral choices that easy for us. When he was preparing *The No Asshole Rule: Building a Civilized Workplace and Surviving One That Isn't,* Robert Sutton reports he was repeatedly challenged by Silicon Valley leaders who asked him, "What about Steve Jobs?" to the point where he reluctantly added a chapter called "The Virtues of Assholes." He concedes that judicious displays of irrational anger have their uses—fear of humiliation can be a motivator for employees if it's balanced with the hope of praise, and a well-timed tantrum can get you a boarding pass at the last minute from uncooperative airport staff. And there are fields where behaving like an asshole offers a clear career advantage, such as professional wrestling and the law. Certain law firms encourage a hardball style that can cross over into what Sandra Day O'Connor has called legal Ramboism. As a former federal judge who became a partner at a notoriously aggressive Wall Street law firm said, "At Skadden Arps . . . we pride ourselves on being assholes. It's part of the firm's culture."

Still, nobody would argue that being an asshole is essential to business success. The books on leadership that line the business sections of Barnes & Noble offer career models to suit every personality type. One can take one's cues from successful leaders ranging from Bismarck and Golda Meir to Nelson Mandela and the apostle Paul, not to mention Generals Lee, Grant, Custer, and Attila the Hun. With that choice before them, the managers who make for the shelf that holds books on Patton and Jobs aren't settling on assholism as a career expedient, they're looking to justify their predilection for it. Few people become assholes reluctantly.

In any event, few of the people who bought Isaacson's biography were looking for tips on becoming masters of the universe or pretexts for rationalizing their own arrogance. And the stories Isaacson tells about Jobs' assholism are different from the ones that hagiographic biographers tell about Patton. They often demonstrate a capacity for irrationality, spitefulness, and petulance that had little to do with any psychological jujitsu: firing a manager in front of an auditorium of people; short-changing Steve Wozniak on a bonus in the early days of their partnership; taking credit for the ideas of others; screaming, crying, and threatening when the color of the vans ordered at NeXT didn't match the shade of white of the manufacturing facility; and launching savagely into anyone who aroused his displeasure. (I know of one person who says he quit his high-level job at Apple because he got tired of wiping Jobs' spittle off his glasses.) True, the Patton of historical fact was by most accounts even worse: a full-blown prick, sadist, and suck-up detested by both his superiors and his subordinates. But most of that has been left out of the story that made Patton an epitome of brilliant leadership, whereas Jobs' pathological behavior is an essential element in his myth.

So it says something that Jobs' assholism hasn't been re-touched for public consumption the way Patton's was. That has a lot to do with the anti-heroic temper of the times; we demand all the dirt, especially on our heroes. But it also suggests a different idea of what makes these asshole achievers compelling, even to those with no interest in emulating them. Jobs' tantrums and rants don't evoke the resolute toughness of a Leader of Men so much as the temperament that we associate with creative genius. He styled himself as an artist rather than a businessman, the turtlenecked begetter of the cool exuded by the company's iStuff. That was a credible posture in an age in which people found it natural to compare the launch of the iPhone to the previous generation's Woodstock, and it seemed to license the prodigal shittiness that goes with being a Bernini, a Picasso, or a Pound—or, for that matter, a Robert Plant. One reviewer of the Isaacson book compared reading it to "going backstage at a Led Zeppelin concert in the seventies and seeing your heroes wasted, and babbling like babies, surrounded by bimbos." Indeed, Jobs was a rock star, in a sense that Bill Gates couldn't possibly be, not just because he was idolized, but because he was one of those people like Jim Morrison, Kanye West, and the Metallica guys, whose behavior as flaming assholes is taken as evidence of being exceptional enough to be able to get away with it.

. . .

Donald Trump comes closer than anyone else to being the archetype of the species; crossing genres, he exemplifies all the ways an asshole can capture our attention. He's in a different league from Patton or Jobs, whose assholism is perceived relative to their other achievements—they'd be remembered even if they had been even-tempered and self-effacing, though perhaps not the subjects of a best-selling biography or an Oscar-winning biopic, whereas Trump would have no more claim on our attention than Harold Hamm, Charles Ergen, Dannine Avara, or most of the other hundred-odd Americans who have more money than he does.

But Trump is a pure asshole in a way that very few people are ever a pure anything, as one dimensional as the villain in a Batman movie. Everything he says reveals the workings of a hermetically self-referential mind. Here he is explaining his objections to gay marriage:

> It's like in golf. A lot of people—I don't want this to sound trivial—but a lot of people are switching to these really long putters, very unattractive. It's weird. You see these great players with these really long putters, because they can't sink three-footers anymore. And, I hate it. I am a traditionalist. I have so many fabulous friends who happen to be gay, but I am a traditionalist.

Not even Stephen Colbert could have come up with that; whatever else can be said about Trump, he writes his own stuff.★

★Colbert did try to riff on Trump's gay marriage disquisition, in a segment extending the logic to other issues. On the debt ceiling: "It's bad. Like almond butter. They're making butter out of every kind of nut these days. What's wrong with peanut butter? The debt ceiling." That nailed the Ionesco-like non sequitur of Trump's remark, but not its weirdly inapt self-reference.

And controversial as he is in other regards, no one disputes that he's an asshole, though people have very different reasons for finding that compelling. Some regard him with *de haut en bas* disdain. In its heyday in the 1980s, *Spy* magazine made a fetish of his arriviste coarseness with the recurrent epithet "short-fingered vulgarian" (in retrospect, the "Not our class, dear" condescension of that phrase is a reminder of how tricky it is to deride an asshole from above). Others take pleasure in seething at his outrageousness. His presidential foray in early 2011, with its opportunistic rekindling of the birther dementia, briefly made him Topic A not just on the right but on the left—at the *Huffington Post*, mentions of Trump trail only those of Sarah Palin, who has been at the game much longer. At the time, even his online supporters conceded that he was an asshole, though they either looked past it or saw it as a plus. To some it meant that he was someone who would get the job done, à la Patton; to others that he wouldn't mince words in letting the world know what an asshole Barack Obama is:

> I will vote for him. The guy might be an asshole but the economy needs a fucking businessman at the helm.

> I will vote for Trump, precisely because he is a jerk, but a jerk who knows when he's getting screwed on a deal, and will make sure it is America that comes out on top.

> Trump may be an arrogant asshole but he says what he thinks.

> He says what so many ppl are thinking but is afraid to say it because of PC. trump is so fearless and does not give a dam

about what ppl think about him. most ppl are afraid to speak
their mind and say what they really believe because they will
be called racist bigoted etc.

Trump's preeminence in this line testifies to his mastery of
the mechanisms of publicity. Apart from Colbert, no one in
public life understands better than he how engaging assholism
can be, both in real life and in its broadcast simulacra. *The Apprentice* epitomizes the genre of reality television built around
situations in which people can be abusive to others who have
willingly consented to take part in return for money or
celebrity. Every episode arcs towards a finale that gives the
viewers the opportunity to watch a powerful man acting like
an asshole towards his supplicants, dispatching the losing
competitor with a brisk, "You're fired." The phrase is supposed to evoke the pitilessness it takes to survive in "the ulti-
mate jungle," but we don't actually feel much compassion for
the losers. They've fought to get there, after all, and any resid-
ual sympathy we might have had for them is dissipated in the
final boardroom scene where they're incited to act like assholes themselves, selling each other out in an effort to be
spared the axe. And anyway, "fired" here really means "playing
a subordinate role in the rest of this season's episodes." So
there's none of the vicarious outrage we might feel watching
a movie of the week that depicts Leona Helmsley summarily
discharging a busboy who spilled some tea in her saucer.

Those scenarios are reproduced, with variations, across
many of the genres of reality television, from *American Idol* to
What Not to Wear to Gordon Ramsay's *Restaurant Makeover*
(which offers, Gina Bellafante said in the *New York Times*, "the

thrill of . . . witnessing someone so at peace with his own arrogance").* In each instance, the format keeps the "reality" close enough to the actual so that the asshole's behavior is distressing to his targets without ever reaching so deep into their lives that it becomes genuinely disturbing to the viewer. They allow us to enjoy the spectacle of social aggression without experiencing any vicarious moral risk, in the same way that "dare" shows like *Fear Factor* allow us to watch contestants attempt to jump from one building to another without any real physical danger. On the contrary, our indignation over the behavior of the designated assholes on the job-search shows like *The Apprentice* and the documentary-style shows like those in the *Real Housewives* franchise isn't diminished by knowing how much of it is engineered by the producers or simulated for the camera. It's the same suspension of disbelief that makes possible the Comedy Central roasts, in which some celebrity, ideally a high-profile asshole himself, winces good-humoredly as comedians who have never met him take turns making pointed put-downs at his expense. ("When Trump bangs a supermodel, he closes his eyes and imagines he's jerking off.") There have been eras that took a far more intense interest in spectacles of cruelty than ours, but none that was so transfixed by watching people act like assholes.

That fascination is fed in equal parts by our fantasies of rock star self-indulgence and the resentments and anxieties

---

*In a class of its own is the brilliantly conceived *Parking Wars,* which tracks the employees of the Philadelphia Parking Authority as they ticket, boot, and tow cars and registers the responses of their owners in a situation that would bring out the asshole in any of us.

that assholes evoke. Both are popular themes in recent cinema. I'm not thinking so much of the innumerable comedies and dramas that feature assholes as their stock villains, but of movies in which the assholes are the focus of dramatic interest. Some of these are tales of asshole redemption, like *Rain Man* and all those other Tom Cruise vehicles. Others are more equivocal about the condition, like *The Company of Men*, *The Politician*, *Greenberg*, *Margin Call*, and *Rules of Attraction*, as well as the mean-girl movies like *Heathers* and *Mean Girls* itself, which break new generic ground. Meanwhile, television has made a mini-industry of the dirtbag sitcoms that I mentioned earlier. And one should make a special place for *The Office*, especially the original version with Ricky Gervais, which created one of the most incisive modern portraits of the asshole's clueless self-delusion. Gervais' David Brent elicits contempt and irritation, pity, even affection—a sign not so much of the complexity of the character but of how conflicted we are about the type he personifies.

· · ·

Some of these assholes are just old curs warmed over, but others are creatures new to film. *The Social Network*, for example, could have been subtitled *Asshole 2.0*. There are obvious resemblances between Mark Zuckerberg and Steve Jobs as driven high-tech creators, but the character of Zuckerberg created by Aaron Sorkin and David Fincher (which by all accounts is substantially different from the real Zuckerberg) belongs to a different genus of assholes. No one would be tempted to describe him as a "master of psychological manipulation," as *Newsweek* did Jobs; he's arrogant, self-absorbed, and insensitive to the point of near-autism. In the opening scene, he preens and condescends to his girlfriend, Erica, in a Cambridge bar ("You don't have to study . . . You go to BU [Boston University]"). She tells him he's an asshole, breaks up with him, and walks out. As if to prove her right, he goes back to his dorm and posts some unflattering and sexist remarks about her on his blog, then, in a misogynistic follow-up, creates the "Facemash" application that allows people to rank the women students for hotness. Later we see him cutting out his best friend, who put up the money for the project, and responding with prodigal snottiness to a lawyer who's deposing him:

> GAGE: You don't think I deserve your attention. . . .
> ZUCKERBERG: You have part of my attention. You have the minimum amount. The rest of my attention is back at the offices of Facebook, where my colleagues and I are doing things that no one in this room, including and especially your clients, are intellectually or creatively capable of doing.

Only in an incongruously mawkish final scene does Zuckerberg reveal a dim awareness of his isolation and loneliness, as he sits alone at a conference table in the offices of his lawyers and sends a Facebook friend request to his former girlfriend, Erica, then keeps compulsively refreshing the page to see if there's a response. All of a sudden he's pathetic, and for the first time strikes us as a possible object of sympathy. "You're not really an asshole," his lawyer, Julie, has told him, but what the scene really shows is that he's *only* an asshole, not an unmitigated shit like most of the other characters—the slick hustler Sean Parker, the supercilious and self-infatuated Winklevoss twins who accused him of stealing their idea.

That last scene put several critics in mind of Charles Foster Kane's "Rosebud," and it seems to set the movie in the long line of American stories that show successful figures repaid for their unchecked ambition with loneliness. The scene is obviously meant to leave the audience with the consoling thought that it profiteth a man nothing if he gains the world but loses his soul mate. But there are no real film antecedents for the figure of the emotionally stunted nerd billionaire (a very far cry from Mickey Rooney in *Young Tom Edison*), just as there are no media precursors of the digital culture that seems to many to foster a kindred sense of disconnection and casual meanness. Or at least that's the perception of many people in the generation of Sorkin and Fincher, who were in their late forties when the film was made. They obviously meant for their Zuckerberg to personify the digital culture, as they signaled in the ambiguous title *The Social Network*. That's how Zadie Smith read the story in the *New York Review of Books*:

> Shouldn't we struggle against Facebook? Everything in it is reduced to the size of its founder . . . Poking, because that's what shy boys do to girls they are scared to talk to. Preoccupied with personal trivia, because Mark Zuckerberg thinks the exchange of personal trivia is what "friendship" *is* . . . We were going to live online. It was going to be extraordinary. Yet what kind of living is this? Step back from your Facebook Wall for a moment: Doesn't it, suddenly, look a little ridiculous? *Your* life in *this* format?

But that's not how people who grew up with Facebook see either Zuckerberg or his creation. When I talk to Berkeley undergraduates about the movie (which they've apparently all seen), they acknowledge that Zuckerberg behaved badly, but they don't see him as the alien and alienating figure that Sorkin and Fincher made him out to be—he's a routine sort of jerk, and if they have it in for him, it's more often because of Facebook's privacy policies than any of the wrongs committed by his movie avatar.* Nor would they recognize either Facebook or themselves in Smith's description of the online world. They don't see their walls and profiles as the places where they live their lives, just as one of the many venues, material and immaterial, where they circulate. And they're quite clear on the difference between friends and "friends." As one student of mine wrote, after describing the assortment of postings on his Facebok wall from classmates, acquaintances, and already forgotten high-school chums, "If I thought this was a representation of my actual life, I'd need to reevaluate it pronto."

In the same way, digital natives aren't as disturbed as their parents are by the snark and assholism endemic in the online world, not because the perpetrators aren't assholes, but because they're relatively harmless ones. It's a curious feature of the age that the forms of assholism that people find most

*For that matter, young aspirants to the start-up culture—which includes about three-quarters of my students, as best I can tell—find Zuckerberg a much more compelling career model than Jobs, who for all his personal unconventionality lived out his working life in a traditional corporate context. They're generally less interested in building the next Apple than in doing a start-up that builds apps for the present one.

alarming tend to be those that have less drastic effects on their daily lives. Abusive blog comments are easier to ignore or shrug off than rude remarks from people behind you in the line at the DMV. But for just that reason, the more remote and impersonal forms of assholism are easier to engage in without rippling one's conscience too much. And while these activities don't generally inflict the personal injuries that assholism can at work or school, they can be enormously destructive of the fabric of public life—the problem I started out with, and that I'll come back to now.

chapter eight

The Assholism of Public Life

The political can derive its energy from the the most varied human endeavors, from the religious, economic, moral, and other antitheses … What always matters is only the possibility of conflict.

—Carl Schmitt, *The Concept of the Political*

JESUS LOVES COWS ON A SESAME SEED BUN

I ABORTED JESUS ON MY WAY TO THE GAY BAR

—T-shirts on sale at cafepress.com

Political Assholes, Political Assholism

A list of assholes who personify the Zeitgeist wouldn't be complete without someone drawn from politics or the political media. Survey respondents consistently rank those areas as the most uncivil of American life, ahead of professional sports, Hollywood, the music industry, and even traffic. Trump technically qualifies, it's true, but his reputation as an asshole was firmly established before his dalliance with politics began. For a truly exemplary figure you'd be better off picking one of the political broadcasters who have built careers around the spectacle of assholism. To judge from the energy they give to preening, sneering, and bullying their guests and callers, a lot of these people are personally assholes, particularly the most successful ones—in talk radio, as in baseball, nice guys finish at the bottom of the division. In that regard, the assholes on political talk radio and cable news aren't different in kind from the ones you see on reality shows; in fact you could think of political broadcasting as just another subgenre of reality television. What makes politics different, is that its assholism isn't simply a matter of rudeness or personal arrogance. It's a rhetorical style aimed at creating a sense of solidarity and partisan identity, and it works off a different dynamic.

At a talk Ann Coulter was giving at the University of Ottawa in 2010, a seventeen-year-old Muslim student asked her how Muslims are expected to travel if they shouldn't be allowed on airplanes, as Coulter had earlier suggested. "Take a camel," Coulter responded. Not surprisingly, the remark created an uproar, and Coulter's subsequent talk had to be cancelled. It was clearly an asshole thing to say, but not exactly in the everyday sense of the word. Coulter defended it as "satire," as she often does, but she doesn't actually satirize anything, unless it's her own outrageousness—this isn't like *South Park* or *Thank You for Smoking*. And while she clearly had no qualms about offending Muslims, her real object was to outrage liberals who disapprove of racist remarks, and titillate her admirers in the process.

Political assholism is a variant of anti-assholism. But in this case you aren't responding to a specific person or a specific insult, the way you are when you give the finger to someone who cuts you off on the highway. In fact you don't really care if any particular person is actually offended by your action, so long as you and your listeners can imagine the outrage it would engender. The process recalls the infantile pleasures of schoolyard swearing, and it's not surprising that conservative audiences often greet Coulter's remarks with the titters and giggles that are the sound of unconscious material bubbling to the surface. That was the response to the crack she made to a conservative group in 2008: "I was going to say something about John Edwards, but it turns out that you have to go into rehab if you use the word faggot." After she was widely criticized for the remark, even by conservatives, Coulter insisted she wasn't trying to say anything anti-gay, and I don't really think that was her objective. She was just looking for something that would *épater* the liberal bourgeoisie, and if that required presuming that everybody in the room was homophobic, so be it. If she could have achieved the same effect by saying "pee, poo, belly, bum, drawers," she would have gone with that instead.

In some ways, this kind of assholism is close to snark—"a strain of nasty, knowing abuse spreading like pinkeye through the national conversation," as David Denby defines it in a recent book dissecting the attitude. Snark tries to be quippy and droll, and when it's well honed and aimed at a deserving target—Newt Gingrich, John Edwards—it can be very funny indeed. But it's essentially cynical and destructive, asking the reader to share a sense of superiority to its target, often by appealing to familiar prejudices. Snark is Sarah Palin on Obama's pre-politics experience—"a small-town mayor is sort of like a community organizer, except that you have actual responsibilities"—and it's the South Carolina Democratic chairwoman Carol Fowler on Palin: "Her primary qualification seems to be that she hasn't had an abortion." It's the tone that ran through just about everything in *Spy* magazine, and that has become a house style at sites like Gawker, Wonkette, Jezebel, and Deadspin, as well as the day-to-day MO of Gail Collins and Maureen Dowd in the *Times*. And while Denby regards snark as a phenomenon whose native habitat is blogs, op-ed columns, and book reviews, it has colonized the everyday language, too: think of the exclamation *Fail!* and the *um* that announces a sarcastic correction of a gaffe or dumb mistake: "Um . . . Ringo was the band's *drummer?*"

Snark and political assholism are clearly fellow travelers: both are pretexts for nastiness and aggression and both permit one to respond to criticism with the "can't you take a joke?" or "hey, it was satire" defenses.* But snark is generally directed at a specific person—Denby describes its platonic ideal as two teenage girls putting down a friend who's sitting at another table in the cafeteria—whereas the objects of political assholism are often just targets of convenience, like Coulter's camel-riding Muslims. Then too, there's nothing really new

---

*For real satire, listen to the way Bill Maher likes to send up that "can't you take a joke?" defense, using "I kid" as if it excused any remark, however abusive: "Hey, birthers, wanna hear my theory? My theory was that Obama was born in America and you were born with the umbilical cord around your neck . . . Oh, I kid the birthers."

about snark, whereas political assholism is a recent phenome-non. The long history of American political rhetoric can pro-duce plenty of controversialists more venomous than Coulter or Limbaugh, but none who was playing the same game. When Westbrook Pegler referred to Jews as geese ("they hiss when they talk, gulp down everything before them, and foul everything in their wake"), he was giving voice to his gnaw-ing anti-Semitism. When Coulter makes an analogous remark about Muslims, she's only trying to *sound* offensive by the lights of the liberals who don't approve of such talk. We know that she doesn't lie awake seething about Muslims the way Pegler did about Jews.

The Personal Is Political, and Vice Versa

I describe this kind of assholism as political because it's always framed as a finger in the eye of power or propriety. It's an en-demic tone in big-P political discourse, as we saw, but it has also worked its way into everyday conversation, particularly as a response to the politicization of manners associated with "political correctness." When the right first coopted that phrase from the left around 1990, it was as a mocking label for the standards of civility that were being incorporated into university speech codes and curricula—what President George H. W. Bush described in 1991 as "attempts to micro-manage casual conversation [that] invited people to look for an insult in every word, gesture, action." But "political cor-rectness" took on a life of its own after those controversies subsided. It spread beyond the campus, nourished by some egregious cases of bureaucratic overreach, by satires like *Politically Correct Fairy Tales* and by urban legends about schools rebaptizing Easter eggs as "spring spheres" or refusing to let kids wear red and green to school at Christmastime. By the end of the decade "PC" was an all-purpose disparagement for any received liberal dogma, with the implication that it was born out of exaggerated "sensitivity," an unwillingness to acknowledge inconvenient facts, or slavery to fashion. (By a happy accident, the word *correct*, which for the old-school Marxists who first coined *politically correct* meant simply exact or true, can also mean *comme il faut*, as in "the correct fork to use with fish," which is how the right reinterpreted it in their version of the phrase.)

To describe yourself as "politically incorrect" is to stake a claim to being plainspoken, independent minded, and courageous—in effect, to say that you're authentic, not an asshole. A remark that would once have stamped you as a boor can now be defended as a blow against fashionable orthodoxy. As the Irish critic Finian O'Toole wrote in 1995:

> We have now reached the point where every goon with a grievance, every bitter bigot, merely has to place the prefix, "I know this is not politically correct, but . . ." in front of the usual string of insults in order to be not just safe from criticism, but actually a card, a lad, even a hero. . . . Anti-PC has become the latest cover for creeps. It is a godsend for every sort of curmudgeon and crank.

Back in 1995, for example, Robert Novak was guest-hosting the Larry King show with Senator Jesse Helms as his guest. A caller from Alabama came on the line and said, "Mr. Helms, I know this might not be politically correct to say these days, but I just think that you should get a Nobel Peace Prize for everything you've done to help keep down the niggers." (Helms, weirdly, responded, "Thank you, I think.") For that caller, the allusion to political correctness was merely a cover for airing his racism undiluted. But often the point is the show of defiance itself, and the person disparaged by the remark is merely a collateral victim, like the student at whom Coulter directed her "Take a camel" line. The offender isn't always a "bitter bigot," as O'Toole puts it. Often he's merely a bigot of opportunity who's trying to play the lad, a brash young layabout acting up for the benefit of his mates.

Dekes, Yale Men, Perfect Assholes

The claim to be politically incorrect was initially a response to the cultural left's insistence that "the personal is political," as feminists put it—as if to say "You want political? I'll show *you* political." If the codes of polite interaction are rooted in politics, then it becomes a political act to reject them. That contention was introduced to justify some of the reassertions of masculine privilege that I mentioned earlier. A lot of what has been called backlash is really just the resurfacing of an unrehabilitated beer guy culture that didn't have any explicit beef with feminism as such. But it could be given a political cast, particularly when it surfaced in elite contexts where feminism itself was a prominent force. There was the incident at Yale in 2009 that I mentioned earlier, when the Zeta Psi fraternity had its pledges pose in front of the Yale Women's Center holding a sign that said "We Love Yale Sluts." Then in the following year, the Yale Delta Kappa Epsilon chapter marched its pledges to the freshman women's dorms chanting, "No means yes, yes means anal." The stunt led Yale to suspend the fraternity, an action that critics on the cultural right denounced as a capitulation to a campaign by militant feminists and "PC campus administrators" who were trying to stifle the members' First Amendment rights. Granted, the critics said, the chants were in poor taste, but the students weren't actually advocating rape, merely satirizing, in an admittedly crude way, the ambient campus climate of political correctness. And isn't it the very purpose of free speech to protect the expression of ideas that are provocative, disturbing, and unorthodox?

Not that anybody really thought the Dekes had contrived the exercise as a satirical performance piece. They were just looking for a way to make their pledges act like obnoxious assholes in public, as Dekes have been doing since the day when George W. Bush was a member, and the anti-feminist slogan served to give them political cover for it. What was innovative wasn't the sophomoric assholism of the Dekes, but the postgraduate assholism of cultural conservatives who depicted the midnight chanting as an intervention in the marketplace of ideas, aimed not at the women in the freshman dorms but the feminists at the Women's Center (who, the *Yale Daily News* reminded its readers, "spent their time painting murals of their own vaginas"). The whole affair could only have happened in an age in which acting like an asshole can be invested with political moment. If the same thing had taken place in W's day (supposing Yale was accepting women undergraduates back then), it's unlikely that the First Amendment would have figured in the subsequent discussion. The fraternity and its members would have been briskly micromanaged off the campus on the unappealable grounds of end-stage loutishness. But then fifty years earlier, W and his fellows would never have chanted that in the first place (can you imagine what mom and dad would have said?). They would have been laddishly pilfering panties, not reciting paeans to anal penetration. Kids today!

It's true there are any number of legitimate gripes that can begin with "This may not be the politically correct thing to say." There were and are an awful lot of progressive prescriptions that deserve to be received with rolled eyes—not least the ever-changing list of approved denominations for constituencies defined by race, gender, ethnicity, sexual orientation, and physical condition, which was the *casus belli* when the whole controversy erupted. Sometimes the reason for beginning a sentence with "This may not be the politically correct word to use" is honest perplexity, especially if you haven't been keeping up. What *are* we calling them now? And "PC" has been given so wide a brief these days that the "political" part often means nothing more than "conventional." It isn't odd to find people saying things like "It's not politically correct to say that the Packers will-out-and-out whip the Giants on Sunday" or "It may not be politically correct to say it, but 64-bit Linux running on commodity hardware powered by AMD won't smite the midrange dinosaurs." (Even PCs have their PC.) The phrase is even used, if not that frequently, to refer to departures from orthodox conservative thinking. "A little political correctness never hurt anybody," a *Chicago Herald* columnist said in applauding the Miami Marlins after they suspended their manager Ozzie Guillen for saying favorable things about Fidel Castro in April of 2012.

Still, to paraphrase what John Stuart Mill said about the stupidity of the Tories, while not all people who claim to be politically incorrect are assholes, it's exactly the sort of thing an asshole is apt to say. The phrase itself implicitly acknowledges that; in its own way, describing a remark as politically incorrect can be a backhand acknowledgment that it really is an asshole thing to say. Indeed, the notion of political incorrectness couldn't have arisen until after most of the linguistic reforms of the cultural left had been accepted as just. By 1990 or so, *gay*, *African American*, *disabled*, and *Hispanic* were obligatory in polite use, while *racist*, *sexist*, and later *homophobia* had become universal disapprobations. That's why Coulter's "faggot" remark could evoke a sense of naughty pleasure when a few decades earlier, it would simply have sounded coarse.

• • •

It's true that the vast majority of Americans profess to take a dim view of political correctness, especially when it's described as such. In a 2011 Rasmussen poll, 79 percent of Americans said that political correctness was a problem.* But by definition, after all, political correctness involves an *unreasonable* imposition on expression; not many people would ap-

---

*The wording of the item was hardly neutral: "Some people think that government officials too often override the facts and common sense in the name of political correctness. Is political correctness a problem in America today?"

peal to political incorrectness to defend that guy who called the Larry King show to talk about keeping the niggers down. It's only in highly partisan quarters that *politically incorrect* has taken on a life of its own as the name of a comprehensive, totalizing worldview, like medieval Catholicism or the *Grand Larousse*. For those people, it has become a catch-all for a collection of ideas that were never perceived as having a political significance before the right took exception to them—not just about evolution, climate change, and the Constitution, but about the relative cultural importance of Bobby Vinton and Bob Dylan (in *Human Events*, Jonathan Leaf notes that Vinton had four number-one hits in the so-called radical sixties while Dylan had none) and whether English literature can be said to have begun with *Beowulf* (it used to, says the *Politically Correct Guide to English and American Literature*, "before PC professors decided that heroism is irrelevant to modern life"). We've come to the point where someone can announce in complete earnestness, "This may not be the politically correct thing to say, but as Conservapedia notes, the instantaneous transmission of Newtonian gravitational effects contradicts special relativity."

People talk about this effect with phrases like "alternate reality" and "living in a bubble"; the social psychologist Jonathan Haidt likens it to William Gibson's "consensual hallucinations," which became the premise of *The Matrix*. All ideologies share that tendency to different degrees: the desire to purge their world pictures of things that are inconsistent with their moral vision. But the cosmology evoked by "political incorrectness" is singularly broad and contrarian. You have the sense that often the point is not so much the hallucination as the consensuality—the sense of collective identity that comes of defining one's beliefs in explicit opposition to the other guy's, far beyond anything that one's political or theological commitments would militate for. Regnery's *Politically Incorrect* guides are strewn with pull-quotes and call-outs to remind readers that every statement in the book is a refutation of some liberal canard, something that your professors don't want to tell you: "Books you're not supposed to read" (e.g., Burke's speeches); "Movies you're not supposed to watch" (e.g., *On the Waterfront*); "Guess what?" ("Greek philosophy was born in a men's club").

The effect of this is to assholize the whole of human knowledge. If everything you've been taught is the product of liberal mendacity, then there's no proposition—about history, art, law, biology, even climatology and physics—that you're obliged to believe, and no argument you're bound to accept. Assholization turns belief itself into a matter of solidarity as much as plausibility. Do they really believe that? It's like asking me whether I really believe the Giants runner was really picked off at first while I and thirty-five thousand other fans at AT&T Park are yelling at the asshole umpire who made the call.*

---

*There are plenty of comparable phenomena on the left, too. Alongside of Regnery's *Politically Incorrect Guide to American History* (a "far-right assault on the truth," as the conservative historian Ron Radosh put it), one could put Howard Zinn's influential *People's History of the United States*—"bad history, albeit gilded with virtuous intentions," the historian of populism Michael Kazin has called it, which "reduces the past to a Manichean fable." If there's a difference here, it's that left writers like Zinn don't assholize the right so much as demonize them; they're too earnest to take the same pleasure in being jerks about it.

T-Shirt Ideologies

This Manichean view of reality is a partisan taste, and so is the rhetorical maneuver of assholism that accompanies it. Indeed, political assholism is just a way of giving flesh to the political identity that flourishes among intense partisans, even if others find it entertaining to tune in from time to time. Despite the ubiquitous talk of an America riven by the culture wars into blue and red nations, there's a lot of evidence to suggest that mass polarization is exaggerated; as the political scientist Morris Fiorina puts it, "No battle for the soul of America rages." Polarization, in that view, is restricted to political elites and to partisan activists. There's some debate over the details of that thesis, partly because polarization itself looks different according to whether you examine voting preferences, party affiliation, opinions on the issues, or the geographic and social sorting that has left more Americans huddled in politically like-minded clusters and communities. But one thing is clear from the rhetoric alone: people who are highly partisan and engaged are likely to construe their political identities differently from others. If you spend a lot of time and energy listening to political broadcasts, participating in Internet discussions, and attending political events—all venues where the rhetoric of political assholism is heavily deployed—it's going to have an effect on the way you see yourself.

If I stress the role of political assholism on the right, it's because that's where it's more systematic and developed, to the point of having become idiomatic. But the underlying principle shapes the identities of partisans on both sides. It's implicit in those T-shirts that websites offer: "Offend a Liberal" or "Offend a Conservative," both continuing with the slogan "Use facts and logic":

> Need a cool, right-wing shirt for the next Tea Party event, town hall meeting, or just to annoy a liberal? . . . Well, pick up some Second Amendment–friendly, anti-Obama, conservative apparel and stickers, but watch out—the Department of Homeland Security may be watching you!

> The Annoy a Conservative, Think for Yourself t-shirts will really tick off any fascist neocon who crosses your path. Liberals are well known for having diverse opinions and being able to think for themselves, whereas conservatives must ask their leaders or their preachers for guidance. These t-shirts are a funny way to show the Republicans what you think of them.

Those shirts dramatize how political identity can arise out of your contemplation of the indignation you arouse in the assholes on the other side. That's the point of slogans like "Proud to Be Everything the Right Wing Hates" and "Proud to Stand for Everything Liberals Hate" or of "Annoy a Liberal: Take Personal Responsibility" and "Annoy a Conservative: Help Someone." Or you can taunt the other side by boasting of an exaggerated attachment to some value they find odious about yours, with slogans like "Gun Control Means Using Two Hands" or "You Say *Commie* Like It's a Bad Thing." One way or another, each side is framing its identity by opposition to the assholes on the other. You wouldn't want to assume that the consumers of these things are representative of any-body's base, but their very crudeness makes the rhetorical mechanisms clear.

The left–right parallels are obvious, too, in the puerile nick-names used by radio hosts and in the comment threads of blogs and articles, whether for each other (libtards, dumb-ocrats, repugnicans, repukes), for public figures (Dumbya, Slick Willie, Shillary, Michael Moron), or for the media them-selves (lamestream media, "Faux News"). Most of these fall in a long tradition of American political vilification, though not even Lincoln collected remotely as ·many nicknames as Obama has, owing in part to the serendipitous phonetic ver-satility of his name: Obamanure, Obumma, ObaMao, Oblowme, ObeyMe, Obozo, and literally hundreds more. More significantly, there's a uniform tone to the comments on those threads, the one place where liberals and conserva-tives come into regular and deliberate contact. People rou-tinely deplore the "siloing" effect of the Internet, where interlinking creates hermetic discourses closed to opposing opinions, but it works the other way, too: the medium also makes it trivially easy, and safe, to go looking for a political fight:

> Still no explanation from any of you Repug fuckholes on why not ONE Repug member of Congress supports the public option??? Despite the fact more Repubs nationwide support it than are against it by a margin of 47%–42%???

> Steele is nothing but the repugs' token "Niger-ian" and they think they're fooling the people with their phony pc bs!

> Libtard's philosophy—Quick, get as many people on the dole and dependent on the Federal Porkulus as we can, so they'll need us for their daily fix. Then we can ignore the neanderthals who pay for it all and make them pay even more.

It's hard to know who these people are, which needless to say is exactly what they're counting on. Some of them are quite well informed; others are factually, not to mention orthographically, challenged.* But the very fact of their participation suggests that their sense of political identity is touched with assholism; left and right, they're among the people who take the "Offend a ____ " T-shirt slogans to heart.

It's important that these people think of their adversaries specifically as assholes. That's what gives the modern rhetoric of polarization its singular stamp and makes it different from the execrations of other ages. Seeing our antagonists as assholes means, for one thing, that the enmity is personal. But the attacks on Lincoln and FDR were personal, too; this is more specific. To regard somebody as an asshole is to diminish him—the metaphor itself contributes part of that—and to reduce him to an object of contempt rather than fear. It suggests familiarity, as contempt often does; it implies that you've seen under his skin to discern his inauthenticity, his self-delusion, his bogus entitlement, and in particular his pathetic

---

*A 2009 Pew study showed that about 15 percent of adult Internet users have contributed comments on political or social issues, but that proportion increases sharply among younger and better-educated users (among users under thirty and college-educated users it is almost 40 percent). In recent years, though, the Tea Party movement has been drawing a greater number of older conservatives online.

unhappiness. It's striking how important it is to both liberals and conservatives to see the other side as miserable and as envious of the happiness of others. Hence the T-shirt slogans "Annoy a Liberal—Work Hard and Be Happy" and "Annoy a Conservative. Think Hard. Do Good. Be Happy." Unhappiness is the price of dishonesty and self-delusion, which are the hallmarks of the asshole. As one conservative puts it, "If you spend your life seething over a litany of grievances you've created from scratch in your own head, then you're probably going to be an Eeyore instead of floating on Cloud 9." And it implies by opposition that you yourself are happy, fulfilled, and authentic. To be sure, it isn't usually made clear why one's personal happiness should bear one way or the other on the correctness of one's views on immigration or marginal tax rates. (Imagine appealing to a similar logic to demonstrate the truth of Christian Science—"they're happier, aren't they?") But at this level ideologies are validated by one's character: you're wrong because you're assholes, we're right because we're not.*

The great advantage of seeing the other guy as an asshole, in symbolic politics or in real life, is that you have permission to be an asshole yourself; you're not bound by the ordinary

---

*Conservatives often point to surveys that show that more Republicans and conservatives report themselves as being happy than Democrats and liberals do, though a lot of the difference vanishes when income, age, health, and religiosity are factored in. A 2008 study by two NYU psychologists suggested that the ability to perceive inequality as inevitable or just rather than unfair accounts for most of the remaining difference. Or as the conservative Dennis Prager put the point, "Utopians will always be less happy than those who know that suffering is inherent to human existence." He's probably right.

courtesies and rules. Sometimes you can make the point simply by gesturing at that principle. You can array all the moves of assholism on a scale from snippy to snarky to shitty, depending on what's said and by whom. As adolescent T-shirt slogans go, "I'd Rather Be Waterboarding" isn't that high on the offensiveness list, whereas it's more unsettling to hear congressmen at a hearing on the Geneva Conventions making wisecracks about hypothermia and sleep deprivation ("There is not an American mom that is guaranteed eight hours of sleep every night!"). You're not an asshole just for defending the use of waterboarding or even torture, but you may be if you try to turn the controversy into a question of wimpiness rather than morality. That's what makes assholism different from other kinds of personal attacks: you can't assholize the other without in some way assholizing yourself.

Assholism Coordinated

Left and right may sound the same in the comments threads of blogs and news stories, but it's only on the right that that same rhetoric is preserved across a range of media and spheres. What people wear on their T-shirts, see on cable news and on the Internet, and watch in congressional debates are threads of the same extended conversation. That testifies to the success of the partisan media like Fox and the talk radio shows and to the right's skill at coordinating the old and new media, the political establishment, and think tanks. As Theda Skocpol and Vanessa Williams note in *The Tea Party and the Remaking of Republican Conservatism*:

[Fox News] fills only one niche in the ecosystem. Many outlets feed off one another, echoing the same messages day after day. American conservatives have a powerful capacity to cycle messages between national and local sources . . . Ideas and news stories often pop up on conservative talk radio or on influential websites such as the Drudge Report or Andrew Breitbart's site before getting picked up by conservative newspapers and television . . . Once a story is up and running, hosts on local conservative radio talk shows play a pivotal role in keeping discussions going.

The focus and interconnectedness of that ecosystem is very clear on Twitter, where statistical analyses have shown that conservatives are more densely connected, retweet each other much more frequently, and stick to a narrower range of topics than those on the left do. And the uniformity across media isn't just a matter of content but of tone and attitude. Wherever you find them, conservatives are talking about the same stories in the same way. You encounter the same themes and the same language in conservative blogs and tweets, from callers to conservative radio programs, from the commentators and politicians on Fox News. Take a sentence from any one of those settings out of context and it can be hard to tell which of them it came from.

That integration couldn't have taken place without the advent of new media that have filled the space between the public and the private with a host of intermediate levels. The blogs and their comments, the social media, the tweets, the YouTube videos that people post—do they belong to private or public life? Neither, really; most of them inhabit an intermediate space that you could think of as "in public"—not common points of reference that everyone can presume as background but still out there for anybody to see and link to (and if enough people do, the places may become public themselves). What emerges is a single manner of talking about the political that threads its way through all of these settings and media. And unlike the political discourse of John Dewey's time, it can percolate up as much as it flows down.

But on the left the conversations tend to be distinct and separate. Each variety of liberals and progressives has its characteristic voice and rhetoric and doesn't give that much evidence of coordinating with the others—not surprising from a sector that can't even agree on a single name for itself. You can pick out strains of political assholism here, but only in the plural. There's what E. J. Dionne calls the aesthetic radicalism of the academic left, whose doctrinal purity precludes direct engagement with either politics or the English language. There's the sanctimoniousness of the Pacifica Radio progressives that I feel descending on me whenever I cross the Bay Bridge to Berkeley. There's the condescending wonkery of the think-tank progressives, the preciosity of the *Portlandia* vegan hipsters, and the dogged parochialism of the multiculturalists, which Todd Gitlin summed up in the title of a chapter of *The Twilight of Common Dreams*: "Marching on the English Department While the Right Took the White House." There's the fastidious evenhandedness of the So-Called-Liberal-Media, in Eric Alterman's phrase. NPR would not be referring to American waterboarding of suspected terrorists as torture, their ombudsperson explained, "to avoid taking sides and using loaded language in a contentious debate," though she conceded that they might permit the use of the T-word if Americans were being waterboarded by Iranians.

Some of this is true political assholism and some of it is just being an asshole *tout court*, the difference being that it's only the former if it's aimed at reinforcing the political identity of a group. But a lot of it is marginal to the mainstream discourse.* And the rest is too fragmented, too dissonant, or too tepid to make for a single voice. There are conservative politicians, like Gingrich, who sound exactly like Rush Limbaugh, but it's hard to find liberal politicians who sound like Bill Maher, if only because it's hard to find politicians who will own up to the L-word in the first place. And even if you're one of the many people who are convinced that NPR is merely a surreptitiously left-wing counterpart of Fox News, you're not going to confuse the voice of *All Things Considered* with *Democracy Now!*, even in the dark.

That may be one reason why the currents of political assholism seem to run much deeper on the right than on the left. If assholism is a way of staking out a political identity, then it's going to be more prominent where that identity is stronger and more integrated. But it's also linked to the way conservatives and liberals understand the object of politics. When people are asked whether it's more important for a

---

*Or unless it's singled out by the conservative media. Over the last decade the otherwise obscure controversialist Ward Churchill has been mentioned on Fox News four times as often as on all other broadcast and cable channels combined, and ten times as frequently as Noam Chomsky. People who listen only to Fox would be excused for concluding that he's a much more important figure on the left than Chomsky is. He makes for a more exemplary left-wing asshole, anyway.

politician to compromise to get things done or to stand firm in support of principles, liberals opt by around two to one for compromise, whereas conservatives choose standing firm by as much as five to one. (Conservatives, too, are over-whelmingly more likely to say that it's more important for politicians to do what is popular with the voters in their district than to do what they think is best for the nation, which reflects a premium on team loyalty.) You can describe the right's position either as one of intransigence or resoluteness, but one way or the other it has been a dominant story in national politics in recent years. It's an attitude with sectarian overtones, with its stress on Manichean divisions, a totalizing worldview, and an insistence on purity. It takes the modern right far from a traditional conservatism, where compromise and barter were seen as "the foundation of all government, indeed every human benefit and enjoyment, every virtue, and every prudent act," as Burke put it. But it isn't essentially a political position; or rather it suggests a different picture of the nature of politics itself, as a theater of confrontation, a part of the larger spectacle of public assholism. Although you can find strains of that on the left, the genre belongs to the right. It's a spectacle in which the representatives of the other side can only be ridiculed and humiliated, not reasoned with. That's probably why almost all of the most successful right-wing talkers and commentators are belligerent, bullying, or overbearing. O'Reilly, Hannity, Limbaugh, Lou Dobbs, Mark Levin, Glenn Beck, and Michael Savage; they're all very good at what they do, but they're none of them people whom even their most devoted fans would welcome having as brothers-in-law. Meanwhile, conservatives like Dennis Miller and Tucker Carlson, who are more amiable and funnier than O'Reilly et al., have had their programs cancelled for lack of viewership.★

. . .

The 2011–2012 Republican primary campaign was the first time that the electoral politics of the right was fully absorbed into that spectacle. Some were calling it the Fox News primaries, not just because so many of the potential candidates had been on Fox payroll at one time or another, but because almost half of Republican voters said they got most of their information from the channel, which was also the venue where the candidates were obliged to appear to make their case. (Appearing on *Fox & Friends,* Dick Morris said, "You don't win it in Iowa, you win it on this couch.") In fact a lot of voters seemed to be interpreting the whole process as a Fox presentation. Conservatives may have had both ideological and personal reasons for their distrust of Romney, but they also found him wanting in the kind of moxie that the spectacle seemed to demand:

★The exceptions are the affable Mike Huckabee on Fox and Joe Scarborough on MSNBC, though neither is remotely as iconic as Limbaugh, Hannity or O'Reilly—nor, for that matter, are arch-jerks on the left like Keith Olbermann. Jon Stewart plays a wholly different game. He ridicules figures on the right among others, sometimes coming close to acting like an asshole. But his object isn't to delight his audience at the thought of how much he's pissing off his targets, which is what defines political assholism. In fact the right gives a lot more thought to what the left thinks of them than the left does with regard to the right.

"He's too nice a guy. He's too soft," said Bill Lonardo, a retired jewelry company owner who attended an establishment GOP dinner Friday in Nashua. He prefers Gingrich, for the former House speaker's edgier personality. "Abrasive! That's what we need."

What the base really seemed to be looking for was a candidate who was willing to be an asshole, someone who would go after Barack Obama, Democrats, and the media with unsparing bile. So long as a candidate did that with reckless intensity, voters were willing to overlook his other shortcomings, like Cain's lack of experience and Gingrich's surfeit of the wrong kind.

So Republican voters dallied with one implausible candidate after another, in search of a pit-bull champion. For a brief moment early in the campaign, they were even willing to embrace the arch-asshole Trump, not because they thought he had the right temperament, views, or values, but only because he seemed like someone who would take it to Obama relentlessly ("so fearless and does not give a damn about what people think or the names that people will call him," as one supporter wrote). Taking up the birther issue was enough to briefly give Trump a nine-point lead in the polls. That horrified establishment Republicans who saw it as a sure loser in a general election; Karl Rove said it made Trump a "joke candidate," who had put himself "off there in the nutty right." But Republican voters didn't simply want to see Obama challenged and defeated, but publicly arraigned for his otherness and illegitimacy. "Birtherism" wasn't a matter of political principle in the way the debt ceiling was; it was a way to have

Obama disgraced and nullified. That same desire subsequently led voters to briefly light on Gingrich, the *fons et origo* of American political assholism and a candidate whom only Trump could have exceeded in his propensity to go off the rails. Voters had no illusions about Gingrich's character or stability, but they expected that the stream-of-consciousness vituperations that won him the cheers of the primary debate audiences would be equally effective in the general election and show Obama up for the extremist America-hating socialist he is:

> Gingrich is a real snake and he should be treated as a precious specimen able to handle things in a proper way among his fellow politicians, while Romney is just a good businessman. People in Washington are used to having Romneys for breakfast while Gingrich will definitely lunch you before you dine him.

> Newt EVISCERATED the lib media last night. I hope he keeps it up. This election needs to be a back alley, no holds barred death match in order to save this country from the stain and his minions. Too much damage has already been done.

After that, Rick Santorum seemed downright mellow as a conservative champion. True, his charges were no less bizarre than Trump's or Gingrich's—calling Obama a snob for saying he wanted everyone to go to college, implying some uncertainty about the president's religion ("He says he's a Christian"), and claiming that none of the California State universities offered American history courses. It all came very close to assholism, though there was a creeping suspicion he might be saying them not to be outrageous but because he actually believed them.

Trump? Cain? Gingrich? Santorum?—really? True, the American people have on rare occasions chosen a new president whom they considered an asshole, though in modern times only Nixon comes to mind, and 1968 was an exceptional case. (A lot of people thought of George W. Bush as an asshole by 2004, but he was an incumbent then, and just as many people considered Kerry an asshole, too.) But it's hard to think of any previous campaign in which a large group of voters have sought a candidate with just that qualification.

Of course Republican voters abandoned those enthusiasms as quickly as they had taken them up, in the end settling grudgingly on Romney, whose rhetorical assholism is relatively subdued. But the process demonstrated how that clamorous style of political assholism has become the most audible strain in American politics, and helps to explain why people overwhelmingly judge that politics is the most uncivil area of American life. It may be that the most virulent and insistent forms of assholism are a minority phenomenon particular to the sunless thickets of the extreme right and left. There's no question the media have exaggerated the extent of that behavior; it's always the squeaky nail that gets the ink, particularly given the public's appetite for spectacles of assholism. But the popular perception isn't illusional, either. Whether we look at candidates, Congress, partisans, or the media, politics really has become more uncivil, and the rise of political assholism has played a big part in that.

GEOFFREY NUNBERG

The Politics of "Incivility"

There's another reason why people see politics as such an uncivil domain: that's what politicians and political commentators keep telling them. What gave the word *incivility* its singularly modern flavor when it was reinvented in the late sixties was its explicitly political character. From the outset, the word was designed to obscure distinctions between the insults of private and public life, so that the slovenliness and unmannerliness of the hippies, campus protesters, and "ultra-militant feminists" discredited their claims to political participation; their incivility was "more than mere rudeness," their critics stressed. (There was a weird reprise of that moment in 2011, when critics of Occupy Wall Street resurrected "dirty hippies," a phrase that would have disappeared from the language thirty years ago if it hadn't been kept on life support by *South Park*.) The remarkable elasticity of the word *incivility* made it easier to weave a jumble of unlike offenses into a grand narrative of social decline. Incivility isn't a morally natural category like rudeness. The voice of conscience that tells us to refill the photocopier tray has a very different timbre from the one that urges us to refrain from burning crosses on people's yards. But both can figure as incivility in the complaints about its rise.

Since then, the charge of incivility has become a standard weapon in political discourse, a way of delegitimating a person or group or denying their right to participate in debate, as in "Who can talk to people who behave like that?" And in the nature of things, taxing someone for incivility can also be a pretext for engaging in incivility oneself. Structurally, it's just a more elliptical variation on the everyday rebuke "Mind your manners, asshole." In fact the charges and counter-charges of incivility that permeate public life have become one of the most acrimonious and disingenuous forms of political assholism. Given that crossfire, it's no wonder that people find public life so uncivil. When A berates B for his incivility, it's a virtual certainty that one or the other of them is being an asshole.

The rhetoric here is bipartisan. Left and right strike exactly the same notes both in their charges of incivility and their responses to them—not surprising, since the roles tend to alternate with shifts in power and with events. The same conservatives who hammered on the "hate speech" of "rage-filled" Democrats during the Bush administration were warning against the "stifling of vigorous debate" that could result from an unreasonable emphasis on civility when liberals were criticizing the tenor of Tea Party rhetoric a few years later. "Civility equals censorship," Rush Limbaugh said in early 2011. "That's exactly what Obama and the left mean when they start talking about civility. That means shut up!" Change a few particulars, and that could be Paul Krugman back in 2003: "All this fuss about civility is an attempt to bully critics into unilaterally disarming—into being demure and respectful of the president." Both sides go on from there to point out that civility isn't the only thing that matters. "I'm all for good manners but this isn't a dinner party," Krugman says, and Benjamin Demott echoes him: "When you're arguing with a thug, there are things that are much more important than civility." "Civility is important," Sarah Palin says, "but we can't underestimate Americans who are very passionate about finding solutions to the problems that we face. And if that involves some healthy, vigorous debate, then allow it to be so."

That sets the stage for the incivility wars, with each side accusing the other of hypocrisy. From Limbaugh:

> We don't need lectures from uncivil leftists about civility, much less Obama. . . . the left is always on the march, always accusing, always throwing bombs, and the Republicans just sit there and take it?

And from Krugman:

> When Ann Coulter expresses regret that Timothy McVeigh didn't blow up *The New York Times, The Wall Street Journal* laughs it off as "tongue-in-cheek agitprop." But when Al Franken writes about lies and lying liars in a funny, but carefully researched book, he's degrading the discourse.

Both sides *do* do it, if often in different ways, but the point of these charges is rarely just to remark on the ubiquity of the problem. In fact, these charges and countercharges of incivility represent one of the most effective rhetorical strategies in the assholism of public life. They're aimed at showing not just that the other side is uncivil, but that its incivility arises out of an inherent character disorder that overrides other considerations—that to be one of those liberals or one of those conservatives, as the case may be, is to be an asshole by nature.

For those purposes, it doesn't really matter whether the incivility is perpetrated by a political figure or someone who is politically marginal; indeed, if liberalism or conservatism is a mental disorder, then it will produce the same uncivil effect wherever it's found, and any instance of that behavior becomes an occasion for abusing the entire breed. Some Tea Party protestors on Capitol Hill yell "nigger" at Congressman John Lewis and "faggot" at Barney Frank; the columnist and novelist Ian Spiegelman writes on Gawker: "Did we expect better of these brain-washed wood-dwellers? Most of that subnormal crowd spent better than a month's salary to get to DC in order to scream down a policy that would benefit them." The conservative site Breitbart.com posts a video headed "Obama Supporters Call Black Congressional Candidate 'Uncle Tom,' N-Word," which is picked up by several dozen blogs and websites. In the video, the Obama supporters in question turn out to be three tipsy fourteen-year-old African American boys coming out of a concert, but commenters take the occasion to denounce them as "typical liberal trash" and deplore the "hate coming out of the left today." In an article on "liberal incivility" at the *American Conservative Daily*, the patron in a West Hollywood bar who curses at Bristol Palin over her mother's position on gay marriage is described as a "bitter homosexual lib" who "exemplifies the leftist disconnect with civility and who virtually exhales hatred." The only way to draw an ideological lesson from the obnoxiousness of some barroom loudmouth is to embrace a "they're all assholes" theory of political identities, in which case, in the natural course of things, you're going to assholize yourself.

The vagueness and open-endedness of *incivility* makes this game easy to play, by permitting bogus moral equivalences between very disparate offenses. (In that way it's like the related term "racial insensitivity," which can accommodate both Michael Richard's nightclub N-word tirade and Republican National Committee chairman Michael Steele's anodyne utterance of "honest injun.") Not that there aren't prototypical examples of political incivility. You think of people shouting down a member of Congress at a town hall meeting, of talking heads berating and interrupting each other on a cable talk show, or of a Wisconsin Democratic assemblyman shouting, "You're fucking dead!" to a Republican assemblywoman who had just called for a surprise vote. Images like those drive most of the concern about mounting political incivility that shows up in the surveys. But they account for only a fraction of the episodes that figure in the back-and-forth accusations of political incivility, which can include just about any form of behavior that falls short of unconditional deference: describing Sarah Palin as "Caribou Barbie" or imitating her on TV, admitting that one hates George Bush, describing the Republican tax program as idiocy, accusing another Republican candidate of making false statements in a debate, calling bankers fat cats. Yet there's also nothing here some partisans mightn't defend as "necessary to a healthy vigorous debate." How do you distinguish between the incivilities that are good for the democratic process and the ones that corrode it?

People do make valiant efforts to carve out some of the distinctions that "incivility" obscures. The *Economist* distinguishes between the rhetoric that's ballistic—that somehow legitimates violence—and the rhetoric that's merely toxic. There is genuinely menacing rhetoric out there, of course.

You don't have to be a semanticist to discern an overtone of violence when two senatorial candidates speak about "Second Amendment remedies" to America's problems or when people show up at Tea Party rallies bearing signs that say "Warning: If [Senator Scott] Brown can't stop it, a Browning can."

But the "violent rhetoric" for which partisans denounce the other side usually stops well short of inciting people to shoot up city hall. The English language is shot through with idioms and expressions that allude to violence without inciting it, most of which pass without notice unless they're called to your attention. One of the most disingenuous moves in the incivility wars is to treat these expressions with a specious literalism; politics makes Freudians of us all. After Joe Biden told a group of union members, "You are the only folks keeping barbarians from the gates," the conservative magazine *Human Events* described him as having used the occasion to "mock the political opposition in vile terms." The conservative radio talker Mark Levin asks why David Gregory hasn't reported the "violent rhetoric" of Democrats, citing Senator Barbara Mikulski's remark, "This entire debate has included throwing women and children under the bus." In a piece at Media Matters on right-wing reactions to the passage of the health care bill, Eric Boehlert writes about the response of one blogger:

> Progressive politicians heed this warning: "Democrats who crammed this unwarranted bill down the throats of the American people who clearly and overwhelmingly opposed it deserve to be drawn and quartered." That's right, *tortured*.

And MSNBC's Ed Schulz goes after Michele Bachmann for saying that she "wanted Minnesotans armed and dangerous," when the context made it clear she was talking about getting people to inform themselves about an energy tax. ("I'm going to have materials for people when they leave. I want people armed and dangerous on this issue of the energy tax, because we need to fight back.")★

The rational response to any of those charges is "Give me a break!" Nobody left, right, or center really believes for a moment that Mikulski was talking about throwing someone under an actual bus, much less urging that it be done, or that that a conservative blogger was literally calling for Democrats to be tortured. It puts you in mind of second-graders calling each other out to the teacher—"Did you hear what Jimmy said? He said the T-word!"—though the point here is really to stoke a sense of outrage rather than to demand justice. It's purely for the benefit of partisans, as a demonstration that in these games of asshole and anti-asshole, catching the other side out takes precedence not just over truth but over plausibility. The rhetoric of assholism gives us license not just to pretend to believe whatever we need to, and even to flaunt the fact.

★In what had to be the most absurd linguistic overreaction to the Arizona shootings, Democratic congresswoman Chellie Pingree urged House Speaker John Boehner to remove "killing" from the name of what Republicans were calling the "Repealing the Job-Killing Health Care Act." Boehner could have responded that in that context *kill* doesn't convey anything more violent than it does when we talk about killing the lights, a bottle of scotch, or a couple of hours between flights. But he dutifully replaced "job killing" with "job destroying" and "job crushing" in his subsequent remarks, thereby rendering the violence of the metaphor nonlethal.

Anyway, even if you do manage to draw the line at rhetoric that actually evokes violent action, you'll let in much too much of the vilification, venom, and snideness that debases the political process. In the wake of the Arizona shootings, the editors of the *New Republic* tried to distinguish incivility (acceptable) from indecency (unacceptable), and found fault with both sides: "The sermonizing left is failing to acknowledge that political debate ought to be intense, tempestuous, and even rude," they said, while "the complacent right . . . is refusing to take any responsibility for rhetoric that goes perilously far into the realm of insult and innuendo." Like many others, they denounced the "personification" ("personalization" might be the better word) of political differences:

> Demonize opinions but not the people who hold them. The rhetoric of personification leads inevitably to the rhetoric of personal destruction. So despise the beliefs, but not the believers.

But politics has been personal since the time of the Greeks, and often there's good reason for it. Do we want to say that Joseph Welch was out of line in asking Senator McCarthy, "Have you no sense of decency, sir, at long last"? And aren't there collective attitudes, like racism, that deserve to be addressed in the same way? The true breaches of civility involve what we describe as "getting personal" or "making it personal," where you disparage someone's character when other arguments should apply. In fact, "making it personal" could stand pretty well as a definition of political assholism, which is a matter of turning ideological differences into intimate antipathies. But when it comes to cases, it isn't easy to draw that line, particularly when people are at pains to blur it. When Dick Gephardt said during a 2004 Democratic primary debate that George W. Bush was a "miserable failure," the former chairman of the Republican National Committee charged him with "political hate speech." But the challenger who says the incumbent is doing a terrible job isn't implying he detests him—and even if he were, it wouldn't merit the moral opprobrium implicit in "hate speech," which involves hatred of a very different order. Who was really being the asshole here?

There's no simple algorithm for defining incivility. You can't get there just by looking at the content of what's said. That's partly because of the inherent vagueness of the word, along with others like *toxic* and *indecent*. And *incivility* is particularly easy for people to overextend, unchecked by the homey moral intuitions that guide us in using *nasty* or *rude*. Still, we don't have to pin down the meaning of incivility to answer the more basic question: whatever was said, can you defend it as furthering healthy political discussion?

This much at least is clear: no serious political purpose is ever served by acting like an asshole. Assholism by definition can't contribute to a "healthy vigorous debate," since it's designed to deny that very possibility: its modus operandi is to unite one faction in its contempt for the assholes in the other. You're acting like an asshole, for example, if you accuse someone of incivility knowing full well that no neutral observer would interpret his behavior that way. Nobody for a moment hears any "violent rhetoric" when Obama says he's itching for a fight with the Republicans or when Michele Bachmann describes Washington as "enemy lines." The only purpose of a charge like that is to give your own partisans the enjoyment of imagining the irritation it will engender, all the more because it's so transparently phony. It's assholism, too, when you take a bigoted or nasty remark by some random partisan as evidence for the pathological incivility of the other side. (The more inconsequential or marginal the speaker, the greater the implication that "they're all like that.") And lists of random examples of "conservative incivility" and "liberal hate" are generally assholism, too. It's assholism to make a point of Barack Obama's saying, "I've been in fifty-seven states, [with] I think one left to go" or of George W. Bush's "Is our children learning?" Nobody really thinks Obama has forgotten how many states there are or that Bush doesn't know the difference between a singular and plural verb. (What kind of idiot would you have to be to dump a company's stock because the CEO made either of those errors?)

It was assholism for Sarah Palin to charge that Obama was "pallin' around with terrorists"—assuming that she said it in order to arouse her supporters, rather than to convince them it was true. (Bringing up "death panels" wasn't assholism; saying something with the intent of deceiving someone is covered by another moral principle of more venerable lineage.) Nazi comparisons are almost always assholism, but not because they actually taint their target with the paragon of absolute evil. They're usually so patently inapt that only flakes and wingnuts take them literally. When Roger Ailes said that NPR executives were "the left wing of Nazism," he wasn't trying to tar NPR as evil in the eyes of the general public or the Congress, but to signal to others on his team that they owed NPR no courtesy or respect and had permission to be assholes about the organization. The multitude of liberals who found it easy to compare Bush to Hitler were playing a similar game. But bogus charges of making Nazi comparisons are assholism, too, as when David Axelrod describes a Romney campaign strategy as a "Mittskrieg" and the Republican Jewish Coalition drops the H-bomb to rebuke him for using "Holocaust imagery." And while the ubiquitous terrorist comparisons often fall under the Nazi category, it's pure assholism when James Bowman contends in the *New Criterion* that Paul Krugman engaged in "extreme and violent rhetoric" in using "hostage situation" and "blackmail" to describe the Republicans' refusal to raise the debt ceiling in 2011, as if *hostage* and *blackmail* had only trickled into the American political vocabulary after 9/11.

The surge of patently phony indignation from all sides—is there anything more telling of the cheapening of public life, of partisans' willingness to trash their credit as serious people? These aren't really judgment calls. Assholism isn't a vague, hard to validate notion like incivility. We know when somebody's being an asshole, and we can usually recognize it in ourselves, at least after the fact, when we've been playing stupid or working our own crowd or stacking the rhetorical deck. We can tell ourselves that we were being assholes in the name of the Lord, but even so.

• • •

The items in that list hardly exhaust the forms of political assholism—and they certainly don't represent all the forms of incivility that are abroad these days—but they underscore assholism's destructive effects on public discourse, the license it gives to dishonesty and self-delusion. The problem isn't with the moral logic of assholism itself, but with the way it has bubbled up into the public sphere. In the course of our daily rounds, we're frequently reminded how useful it is to have the sentence "What an asshole!" available to us, whether or not we utter it aloud. I suppose someone could argue that the existence of the word itself creates a vicious circle of rudeness, and that faced with an asshole's provocations, we'd be better people if we could resist the temptation to respond in kind. I think of what the Reverend Villars advises his ward in Fanny Burney's *Evelina,* as she is about to visit an imperious relation: "The more forcibly you are struck with improprieties and misconduct in another, the greater should be your observance and diligence, to avoid even the shadow of similar errors." That's what I'd tell my ward, too, in those circumstances, but it's hard to see this as a categorical moral requirement. There are times when being an asshole to someone who is being an asshole is not only a right but close to a moral duty, when you're obliged to say, "Mind your manners, asshole."

I think Kant would have agreed. Making allowances, he wouldn't have objected to saying, "Mind your manners, asshole!" to someone who treats you disrespectfully. Faced with the "insulting attacks of a contemptuous adversary," he wrote in *The Metaphysics of Morals,* you have the right to be derisive in reply, as "a legitimate defense of the respect one can demand from him." If he fails to respect your dignity as a person, that is, you can repay him by disrespecting his, which is in a nutshell the logic of assholism. But he went on to qualify his remark:

But when the object of his mockery is really no object for wit but one in which reason necessarily takes a moral interest, then no matter how much ridicule the adversary may have uttered . . . it is more befitting the dignity of the object and respect for humanity either to put up no defense against the attack or to conduct it with dignity and seriousness.

Or as we might put it, when somebody is being an asshole about a really important matter, then out of respect for the topic alone you ought to refrain from being an asshole back at him and answer instead with the seriousness the question requires. The important business of public life creates an obligation of self-restraint. That doesn't mean you can't be indignant, sarcastic, mocking, scorching, or scathing in response, and it certainly doesn't preclude being entertaining. But you can't play stupid, deliberately misreading what everybody knows are innocuous remarks. You can't ridicule the other side for their cultural traits or consumer habits. And most important, you can't say provocative things to the other side just to titillate your own; that is, just for the pleasure of being an asshole.

To be sure, I can't really see people in general signing on for this, and I don't think it would have a perceptibly uplifting effect on the state of public discourse even if they did. As I've tried to show, the assholism of public life isn't an independent phenomenon or a passing phase. It's an outgrowth of attitudes that first took root some decades ago and that run everywhere through the culture. It isn't likely to be set right even by the concerted efforts of the foundations, school programs, institutes, conferences, and conclaves, and calls for national conversations aimed at addressing a perceived crisis of civility, though one of course wishes them well. Still, there's a lot to be said for forbearance in the face of other people's assholism in public life. For one thing, there isn't actually much of a cost to it, and it may actually be a winning strategy. The surprising thing about political assholism is that it isn't really a very effective political tactic over the long run. It's a good way of creating a loyal media audience and a sense of community among like-minded people. But that isn't the same thing as building an electoral majority, and in that regard assholism actually works against you. The demands that it makes—the necessity of viewing the people on the other side as assholes, the predilection for provocative rhetoric, the sectarian rigidness—are disconcerting to people who aren't disposed to think in that way, even if they're generally sympathetic to your point of view. Then, too, forbearance offers the austere satisfaction of demonstrating true civility, which when you come down to it is basically a matter of abstaining from being an asshole to someone who clearly has it coming. I say "austere," because in my own experience, I have to say, the pleasure has generally proven more theoretical than visceral. But I can console myself that I have more latitude in everyday life, where no categorical moral principle forbids me from yelling *Asshole!* at the guy who cuts in front of me in the exit lane. Even Kant would be with me on that one.

Notes

Chapter 1: The Word

4 **Fifty years ago:** Peter Viereck, *Shame and the Glory of the Intellectuals* (Transaction Publishers, 2007, 1953), p. 313.

4 **A debate audience applauded:** "Rick Perry's Latino problem," *CNN.com*, October 12, 2011, http://bit.ly/mRgenv. Greg Sargent, "GOP Debate Crowd Cheers Idea That Jobless Are to Blame for Their Plight." *The Plum Line blog—Washington Post*, October 19, 2011, http://wapo.st/qaIqwB. Eric Zorn, "Jeers and Cheers Start a Wild GOP Week," *Chicago Tribune*, January 22, 2012.

5 **The typical adherent of the Tea Party right:** Kate Zernike and Megan Thee-Brenan, "Poll Finds Tea Party Backers Wealthier and More Educated," *New York Times*, April 14, 2010. David E. Campbell and Robert D. Putnam, "Crashing the Tea Party," *New York Times*, August 16, 2011.

6 **"Wanna talk about the country's 'First Black President'?":** Comment by thelastvirgil at Kevin Pilley, "Clinton Country," August 7, 2005, http://bit.ly/GQ13rl.

7 **"Usually a political movement":** Michael Tomasky, "Republican Day of Wrath," *New York Review of Books*, September 29, 2011.

8 **"celebrations of meanness and inhumanity":** Charles Simic, "New Hampshire Follies," *New York Review of Books*, February 23, 2012.

9 **Rush Limbaugh managed to achieve a fusion:** Brian Stelter, "Attack by Limbaugh Awakens a 'Stop Rush' Campaign," the *New York Times*, March 2, 2012, online at http://nyti.ms/HGaH2L.

10 **"Next time you're in line waiting":** J. Roycroft, "The Moocher

Class Is Finally Outnumbering the Producers," *The Roycroft Report,* May 9, 2011, http://bit.ly/JWc3od.

11 **"I was driving south on the Meadowbrook":** Comment on democraticunderground.com, January 22, 2007, http://bit.ly/K54ejS.

13 **Public criticisms of someone's grammar:** Alexander Nazaryan, "The Real George Zimmerman's Really Bad Grammar," *New York Daily News* "Pageviews" blog, April 10, 2012, http://nydn.us/J6Q7EK.

14 **"For sheer verbal savagery":** Ron Chernow, "The Feuding Fathers," *Wall Street Journal,* June 26, 2010,.

18 **"a vulgar euphemism for a rectal aperture":** "Bush Draws Rebuke from Gore for a Salty Side," *Washington Times,* September 5, 2000. Maureen Dowd, "Liberties; Minor-League Mouth," *New York Times,* September 6, 2000.

Chapter 2: The Uses of Vulgarity

22 **Still, there's a paradoxical irony:** Pamela Fiori in Jim Brousseau (ed.), *Social Graces: Words of Wisdom on Civility in a Changing Society* (Hearst Communications, 2002), p. 10. Steve Farkas and Jean Johnson with Ann Duffett and Kathleen Collins, "Aggravating Circumstances: A Status Report on Rudeness in America" (Public Agenda, 2002).

24 **Nowadays, in fact, the objection to vulgarity:** James V. O'Connor, *Cuss Control: The Complete Book on How to Curb Your Cursing* (iUniverse, 2006), p. 161. Stephen L. Carter, *Civility: Manners, Morals and the Etiquette of Democracy* (Harper Collins, 1968), p. 68.

26 **None of that is even remotely true:** Erving Goffman, *Forms of Talk* (University of Pennsylvania Press, 1981), p. 98. Robert Musil, "On Stupidity," in Burton Pike and David S. Loft (eds. and trans.) *Precision and Soul* (University of Chicago Press, 1980), 278.

29 **"That guy you went out with is a freakin' jerk":** "Do guys assume an invite always includes sex?," *Cosmopolitan* online, http://bit.ly/zK5UsH.

35 **The specter of class colored the utterance:** "Gore's Summer

Surprise," *Newsweek*, November 19, 2000. Jake Tapper, "A 'major league asshole': In an embarrassing gaffe, George W. Bush insults a *New York Times* reporter," *Salon.com*, September 4, 2000, http://bit.ly/sH9paZ.

35 **The incident provoked a blizzard of commentary:** David Nyhan, "… It wasn't pretty," *Boston Globe*, September 6, 2000. "George W. Bush Makes Personal Attack on New York Times Reporter Adam Clymer," *CBS Evening News*, May 5, 2000.

36 **Meanwhile, Bush's defenders:** Steve Dunleavy, "Way to go George! You tell 'em! *New York Post*, September 5, 2000, 5. Cal Thomas, "Bush remarks not out of line," *Lawrence Journal-World*, September 7, 2000, p. 7B.

37 **Those reactions are automatic:** William Powers, "MEDIA: Anyone but Us," *National Journal*, July 8, 2000. L. Brent Bozell III, "Is Boston Globe Purging Its Sole Un-PC Columnist?" *Insight on the News*, August 14, 2000. Jonah Goldberg, "Bush's Wedg(ie) Issue," *National Review*, September 5, 2000.

38 **"an arrogant and unaccountable priesthood of kingmakers":** Jonah Goldberg, "Bush's Wedg(ie) Issue," *National Review* online, September 5, 2000, http://bit.ly/JhcOui.

39 **Does our language shape our ideas:** Quoted in William Morris and Mary Morris, *Harper Dictionary of Contemporary Usage* (Harper and Row, 1975), p. xix. George Orwell, *1984* (Penguin Books, 1950), p. 309. William Robertson, "Entertaining Book Hails the Power of Language," *Miami Herald*, July 15, 1990, p. 7C.

41 **"If a language provides a label":** Steven Pinker, *The Stuff of Thought: Language as a Window into Human Nature* (Penguin Books, 2007), p. 129.

42 **But sometimes we introduce a new word:** Quentin Skinner, "Approaching historical texts," in William L. Richter (ed.) *Approaches to Political Thought* (Rowman and Littlefield Publishers, 2009), p. 168. Mary G. Dietz, "Patriotism," in Terrence Ball, James Farr, and Russell L. Hanson, *Political Innovation and Conceptual Change* (Cambridge University Press, 1989), p. 187.

43 **"the yuppie beau ideal":** John Bayley, *The Power of Delight: A*

Lifetime in Literature, Essays 1962–2002 (W.W. Norton & Company, 2005), p. 34.

44 **And once you grasp the idea of cool:** Peter N. Stearns, *American Cool: Constructing a Twentieth-Century Emotional Style* (New York University Press, 1994).

44 **"observe the moral life in process of revising itself":** Lionel Trilling, *Sincerity and Authenticity* (Harvard University Press, 1971, 1972), p. 1.

45 **"mighty scoundrel":** Charles Dickens, *Little Dorrit*, Cleartype Edition (Books Inc., 1867, 1868), p. 678.

49 **Yet the words can be decontaminated:** Maureen Dowd, "Liberties; Minor-League Mouth," *New York Times*, September 6, 2000.

52 **At one point Frankfurt compares:** Harry G. Frankfurt, *On Bullshit* (Princeton University Press, 2005), p. 5; http://bit.ly/y7qy51.

Chapter 3: The Rise of Talking Dirty

55 **"Lieutenant (sg) Dove, USNR. A Cornell man":** Norman Mailer, *The Naked and the Dead* (Picador, 1998), p. 238.

56 **Hemingway would have taken to it:** Kenneth S. Lynn, *Hemingway* (Harvard University Press, 1987), p. 382. See also J. H. Willis Jr., "The Censored Language of War: Richard Aldington's Death of a Hero and Three Other War Novels of 1929," *Twentieth Century Literature*, Vol. 45, No. 4 (Winter, 1999), pp. 467–487.

57 **"Philip was a nerd—a chemistry major":** Paul Fussell, *Doing Battle: The Making of a Skeptic* (Little, Brown, and Company, 1996), pp. 61–63.

58 **T. S. Eliot wrote a poem called "The Triumph of Bullshit":** Loretta Johnson, "T. S. Eliot's Bawdy Verse: Lulu, Bolo and More Ties," *Journal of Modern Literature*, Vol. 27, No. 1/2, Modern Poets (Autumn, 2003), pp. 14–25. Dates of all other first citations from J. E. Lighter, *Historical Dictionary of American Slang* (Random House, 1994) and J. Green, *Green's Dictionary of English Slang* (Oxford, 2011).

59 **The Naked and the Dead also provides:** Jesse Sheidlower, *The F Word* (Random House, 1995).

59 **"Indispensable both to those administering chickenshit"**: Paul Fussell, *Wartime: Understanding and Behavior in the Second World War* (Oxford University Press, 1990), p. 95.

61 **Mencken dismissed such words**: H. L. Mencken, *The American Language, Supplement I* (Knopf, 1945), p. 664.

62 **But Victorian profanity was never really intended as blasphemous**: Octavius Brooks Frothingham, *Knowledge and Faith: And Other Discourses* (G. P. Putnam, 1876), p. 10. Ellen Bayuk Rosenman, "Rudeness, Slang, and Obscenity: Working-Class Politics in *London Labour and the London Poor*," in Susan David Bernstein and Elsie B. Michie (eds.), *Victorian Vulgarity* (Ashgate Publishing, 2009), p. 55.

64 **"Run along, asshole—I'm in the merchant marine"**: Paul Fussell, *Wartime: Understanding and Behavior in the Second World War* (Oxford University Press, 1990), p. 90.

64 **The subtext of swearing has always been class**: G. T. W. Patrick, "The Psychology of Profanity," *Psychology Review*, Vol. 8, No. 2, (March, 1901), pp. 113–127. Delavan L. Pierson (ed.), *The Missionary Review of the World*, Vol. 44, No. 1 (January, 1921), p. 600.

65 **The upper-class "dandies" who joined Teddy Roosevelt's Rough Riders**: Michael Kimmel, *Manhood in America, A Cultural History*, (Free Press, 1996) p. 185. Philip Everett Curtiss, "The mucker pose," *Harper's Magazine* (November 1921), p. 662. James Truslow Adams, "The Mucker Pose," *Harper's Magazine* (November 1928), p, 661.

66 **Nor was the use of risqué language the exclusive province of men**: Mary Agnes Hamilton, "Nothing Shocks Me," *Harper's Magazine*, July 1927, p. 152. Oliver Herford, *The Deb's Dictionary* (J.B. Lippincott, 1931).

66 **Ordinary middle-class Americans were slower**: H. L. Mencken, "American Profanity," *American Speech*, Vol. 19, No. 4 (December 1944), pp. 241–299.

67 **When the World War I drama *What Price Glory***: Joseph Wood Krutch. *The American Drama Since 1918: An Informal History*. (Brazillier, 1957), p. 35.

67 The enfeeblement of profanity led some to predict: H. L. Mencken, "American Profanity," *American Speech*, Vol. 19, No. 4 (December 1944), pp. 241–249.

68 "We have lately seen the heroes of a great moral war": H. L. Mencken, foreword to Burges Johnson, *The Lost Art of Profanity* (Bobbs-Merril, 1948), p. 12.

68 "In his effort to carry his realistic portrayal of men at war": Orville Prescott, "The Books of the Times," *New York Times*, May 7, 1948.

69 Even as Prescott was writing: John C. Burnham, *Bad Habits: Drinking, Smoking, Taking Drugs, Gambling, Sexual Misbehavior, and Swearing in American History* (New York University Press, 1993), p. 221. Herman Wouk, *The Caine Mutiny* (Little, Brown, and Company, 1951), p. x.

70 But the new language was chiefly spread: Bernard Augustine DeVoto, "The Easy Chair," *Harper's Magazine*, December, 1948, pp. 98–101.

72 The spread and acceptance of the new vocabulary: Rochelle Gurstein, *The Repeal of Reticence: America's Cultural and Legal Struggles Over Free Speech, Obscenity, Sexual Liberation, and Modern Art* (Hill and Wang, 1998). Agnes Repplier, "The Repeal of Reticence," *Atlantic Monthly*, Vol. 113 (March 1914), p. 298. D. H. Lawrence, *Lady Chatterley's Lover and "A Propos of Lady Chatterley's Lover"* (Cambridge University Press, 1993), p. 334.

74 "would be naturally and habitually used": Thomas C. Mackey, *Pornography on Trial* (ABC-CLIO, 2002), p. 155.

74 "Hence the controversy that began in 2003": David G. Savage and Jim Puzzanghera, "High court may rethink @#★! on TV," *Los Angeles Times*, March 2, 2008. Daniel W. Drezner, "What the F$%& is Kevin Martin Thinking?" *DanielRezner.com*, June 6, 2007, http://bit.ly/HacUnw.

76 "There's one word which Amerika hasn't destroyed": Quoted in John C. Burnham, *Bad Habits: Drinking, Smoking, Taking Drugs, Gambling, Sexual Misbehavior, and Swearing in American History* (New York University Press, 1993), p. 226.

76 **To be sure, that was a minority view on the left:** John H. McWhorter, *Doing Our Own Thing: The Degradation of Language and Music and Why We Should, Like, Care* (Gotham Books, 2003), p. 134. Jerry Rubin, *Do It: Scenarios of the Revolution* (Simon and Schuster, 1970), p. 111. Neil J. Smeisler, *Reflections on the University of California: From the Free Speech Movement to the Global University* (University of California Press, 2010), p. 34.

77 **But however dubious the logic:** Mark Rudd quoted in John C. Burnham, *Bad Habits: Drinking, Smoking, Taking Drugs, Gambling, Sexual Misbehavior, and Swearing in American History* (New York University Press, 1993), p. 226. Jim Dawson, *The Compleat Motherfucker: A History of the Mother of All Dirty Words* (Feral House, 2009), p. 100.

78 **The defenders of the established order:** Humphrey quoted in Henry J. Perkinson, *Getting Better: Television & Moral Progress* (Transaction Publishers, 1996), p. 150. George Will, *One Man's America: The Pleasures and Provocations of Our Singular Nation* (Three Rivers Press, 2008), p. 215.

79 **But whatever their remote etymologies:** Thomas De Quincey, "Second Paper on Murder Considered as One of the Fine Arts," *Blackwood's Magazine,* Vol. 46, November 1839, p. 663. Edward Shils, *The Virtue of Civility* (Liberty Fund, 1997), p. 49.

80 **But when commentators and social critics disinterred:** "The Decline of Manners," *Wall Street Journal,* October 30, 1968, p. 20.

81 **The *New York Times* acknowledged the short-sightedness:** "Crisis Management on Campus," *New York Times,* May 11, 1969, p. 14.

81 **In 2007, when a conservative blog posted a study:** Mona Charen, "Re: Web Nastiness," *The Corner Blog, National Review Online,* March 28, 2007, http://bit.ly/nZusl7.

82 **To evoke civility is to presuppose:** Quotes on civility from: Bruce Evan Blaine, *The Psychology of Diversity: Perceiving and Experiencing Social Difference* (Mayfield Publishing Co., 1999), p. 168. Mark Kingwell, *The World We Want: Restoring Citizenship in a Fractured Age* (Rowan & Littlefield, 2000), p. 9. Don Herrin, "Deep Learning": A Critical Thinking Resource, p. 36, http://bit.ly/H82PWQ. Lydon

Olson, "Lyndon Olson on the Case for Civility," *Texas Tribune*, November 16, 2009.

84 **"applicable to virtually any example of moral or mannerly misbehavior"**: Cheshire Calhoun, "The Virtue of Civility," *Philosophy and Public Affairs*, Vol. 29, No. 3 (Summer 2000), pp. 251–275.

Chapter 4: The Asshole Comes of Age

86 **"You don't need a rectal thermometer to know who the assholes are"**: Quoted in Todd Gitlin, *The Sixties: Years of Hope, Days of Rage* (Bantam Books, 1987), p. 383.

87 **"Is it my imagination or is there a law"**: Paul Dickson, *Slang: The Topical Dictionary of Americanisms* (Bloomsbury Publishing, 2006), p. 262.

88 **The pervasive cultural theme of that period**: Roger Rosenblatt, "The Scariest Time of the Year," *Time*, November 3, 1980. "The Decline of Manners," *Wall Street Journal*, October 30, 1968. Edward Sapir, "Fashion," in David G. Mandelbaum (ed.), *Selected Writings in Language, Culture, and Personality* (University of California Press, 1949), p. 374.

89 **"something that is willfully substituted"**: Otto Jespersen, *Language: It's Nature, Development, and Origin* (Henry Holt and Company, 1922), pp. 299–301.

92 **It was around this time that law enforcement officers**: Norm Stamper, *Breaking Rank: A Top Cop's Expose of the Dark Side of American Policing* (Stamper Nation Books, 2006), p. xi. John Van Maanen, "The Asshole," in Peter K. Manning and John Van Maanen (eds.), *Policing: A View from the Street* (Goodyear Publishing, 1978), pp. 307–328.

94 **the hidden injuries of class**: Richard Sennett and Jonathon Cobb, *The Hidden Injuries of Class* (W. W. Norton & Company, 1993).

96 **"I realized that Harry was the kind of part"**: Quoted in Michael Munn, *John Wayne: The Man Behind the Myth* (New American Library, 2004), p. 308.

102 **"authenticity required defining oneself against"**: Abigail Cheever, *Real Phonies: Cultures of Authenticity in Post–World War II America* (University of Georgia Press, 2010), p. 4.

104 **"Class, conservatives insist"**: Thomas Frank, *What's the Matter with Kansas?* (Macmillan, 2005), p. 114.

105 **"Collectively, we Americans might not know exactly what 'authentic' is"**: John Zogby, *The Way We'll Be: The Zogby Report on the Transformation of the American Dream* (Random House, 2008), p. 163.

106 **"Americans do not see society as a layer cake"**: David Brooks, "One Nation, Slightly Divisible," *Atlantic Monthly*, December 2001.

106 **The yuppie was merely a specific form**: Victor Davis Hanson, "Obama: Fighting the Yuppie Factor," *National Review Online*, August 13, 2010, http://bit.ly/HoLxXY.

109 **"Asshole is the going insult this year"**: Tom Wolfe, "The Street Fighters," *Mauve Gloves and Madmen, Clutter and Vine* (Farrar, Straus and Giroux, 1976), p. 235.

114 **"appeared cynically to conform to codes of behavior"**: Cheever, *Real Phonies,* p. 2.

115 **"a rule of phonies"**: Allen Ginsberg in Gordon Ball (Ed.) *Journals: Early Fifties, Early Sixties* (Grove, 1977), p. 146, http://bit.ly/rZl2oe.

Chapter 5: Men Are All Assholes

119 **the description of a feminist panel**: Franklin K. Ashley, "Job Market at the MLA: Let Them Eat Interviews!" *Change*, March 1975, p. 36.

116 **But Jacobins and bluestockings weren't the only women**: Timothy Jay, *Cursing in America* (John Benjamins, 1992). Gael Greene, *The Cosmo Girl's Guide to the New Etiquette* (Hearst Corporation, 1971).

131 **what the *New Yorker*'s TV critic Emily Nussbaum calls the dirtbag sitcom**: Emily Nussbaum, "Tool Time," *New Yorker*, March 19, 2012.

131 **"My name is Tucker Max"**: Tuckermax.com, http://www. tuckermax.com.

132 **a Yale fraternity has its pledges pose**: Lawrence Gipson, "A Year Later, Little Impact from 'Sluts' Controversy," *Yale Daily News*, February 16, 2009, http://bit.ly/HVWY7q. Kayla Webley, "It's Not Just Yale: Are Colleges Doing Enough to Combat Sexual Violence?," *Time*, April 18, 2011, http://ti.me/HVWzC6.

134 **the five most common modifiers of** *bitch*: Counts made at Corpus of Historical American English at Brigham Young University, http://corpus.byu.edu/coha.

135 **Often the word just suggests spitefulness or abrasiveness**: Karrin Vasby Anderson, "Rhymes with Rich: 'Bitch' as a Tool of Containment in Contemporary American Politics," *Rhetoric & Public Affairs*, Vol. 2, No. 4 (Winter 1999), pp. 599–623.

Chapter 6: The Asshole in the Mirror

137 **"In the early Seventies it seemed that no ex-movement household"**: Todd Gitlin, *The Sixties: Years of Hope, Days of Rage* (Bantam Books, 1987), p. 425.

138 **"For the middle class, that focus was nourished by an alphabet soup of therapies"**: Suzanne Snider, "est, Werner Erhard, and the Corporatization of Self-Help," *The Believer*, May, 2003. Luke Rhinehart, *The Book of est* (Holt, Rinehart and Winston, 1976).

140 **"You taught me to hate myself"**: Jerry Rubin *Growing (Up) at 37*, (Warner Books, 1976), pp. 140–142.

141 **"The spectacle of people paying a couple of hundred dollars"**: "Behavior: est: 'There Is Nothing to Get,'" *Time*, June 7, 1976, http://ti.me/LmdRt7.

142 **"What, after all, does it mean to 'take responsibility'"**: David Frum, *How We Got Here: The 70's, the Decade That Brought You Modern Life* (Basic Books, 2000), p. 136.

143 **"These critiques of cultural effects of the era"**: Daniel F. Piar, "A Welfare State of Civil Rights: The Triumph of the Therapeutic in American Constitutional Law," *16 Wm. & Mary Bill of Rts. J. 649*

(2008), http://bit.ly/GYRdpp. Ronald W. Dworkin, "The Rise of the Caring Industry," *Policy Review*, No. 161 (June 1, 2010).

146 **"from badness to sickness"**: Peter Conrad and Joseph W. Schneider, *Deviance and Medicalization: From Badness to Sickness* (Tempe University Press, 1992).

146 **"But the colloquialization of terms didn't always signal"**: Susan Lee, "A Schlub and a Narcissist," *Forbes*, March 27, 2009. Jeffrey Kluger, "Putting Bernie Madoff on the Couch," *Time*, December 31, 2008.

147 **"a loose synonym for bloated self-esteem"**: Peter Gay, *Freud: A Life for Our Time* (W. W. Norton & Company, 1988), p. 340.

148 **"In terms of psychology, the 'asshole' consists of"**: Jen Kim, "Do Girls Really Love Assholes?" *Psychology Today*, January 19, 2010, http://bit.ly/vNmBft.

149 **After Madoff was exposed**: Stephanie Strom, "Elie Wiesel Levels Scorn at Madoff," *New York Times*, February 26, 2009.

150 **"Hearn remembered Dove's saying to him"**: Mailer, *The Naked and the Dead,* p. 238.

Chapter 7: The Allure of Assholes

153 **And the idea of decline is implicit**: Kyle Wingfield, "Moving Past Our Summer of Incivility," *Atlanta Journal-Constitution* online, September 18, 2009, http://bit.ly/12sKdj.

153 **In a 2002 Public Agenda poll**: "Aggravating Circumstances: A Status Report on Rudeness in America," Public Agenda survey prepared for Pew Charitable Trust, 2002, at http://bit.ly/Hh1ijX. "Civility in America: A Nationwide Study," 2002. Weber Shadwick, http://bit.ly/HVCbPk.

155 **Civility is a matter of appearances**: David Hume, "An Enquiry Concerning the Principles of Morals," in *Enquiries Concerning Human Understanding and Concerning the Principles of Morals*, 3d ed. (Oxford University Press, 1979), p. 261.

155 **In *On Rude Democracy***: Susan Herbst, *Rude Democracy: Civility and Incivility in American Politics* (Temple University Press, 2010) p. 5.

158 **"There's No Escape":** David E. Scherman, "Transistor Craze—There's No Escape," *Life,* November 24, 1961, p. 23.

156 **You could make that point about bullying, too:** Figures from the National Center for Educational Statistics, reported in Nick Gillespie, "Stop Panicking about Bullies," *Wall Street Journal,* April 2, 2012.

157 **"rudeness, stupidity, and indifference":** Anne O'Hagan, "Behind the Scenes in the Big Stores," *Munsey's Magazine,* Volume 22, January, 1900, p. 532.

158 **"The serenading troubadour can now thrum his throbbing guitar":** *The Electrical World: A Weekly Review of Current Progress of Electricity and Its Practical Applications,* Vols. III and IV (W. J. Johnston, 1884), p. 68.

158 **Etiquette columnists of the 1950s:** David E. Scherman, "Transistor Craze—There's No Escape," *Life,* November 24, 1961, p. 23.

159 **"banging out an e-mail is just so easy":** Michael Kinsley, "Cybercreeps Run Amok," *Washington Post,* July 24, 2005.

161 **"If he slapped a soldier":** Alan Axelrod, *Patton on Leadership: Strategic Lessons for Corporate Warfare* (Prentice Hall, 1999), p. xv.

161 **"CEOs, middle managers and wannabe masters of the universe":** Tom McNichol, "Be a Jerk: The Worst Business Lesson from the Steve Jobs Biography," *Atlantic,* November 28, 2011.

162 **"He found that by delivering brutal putdowns of his co-workers":** Alan Deutschman, "Exit the King," *Newsweek,* September 21, 2011.

162 **"At Skadden Arps . . . we pride ourselves on being assholes":** Quoted in Lincoln Caplan, *Skadden: Power, Money, and the Rise of a Legal Empire* (Noonday Press, 1994), p. 147.

164 **Jobs' assholism hasn't been retouched for public consumption:** Carlo D'Este, *Patton: A Genius for War* (Harper Collins, 1995).

165 **"It's like in golf":** Michael Barbaro, "After Roasting, Trump Reacts in Character," *New York Times,* May 1, 2011.

171 **"Shouldn't we struggle against Facebook?":** Zadie Smith, "Generation Why?," *New York Review of Books,* November 25, 2010.

Chapter 8: The Assholism of Public Life

174 **Rank those areas as the most uncivil:** Colette Thayer, "AARP Bulletin Survey on Civility," American Association of Retired Persons, March 2011, http://aarp.us/HCyaO4.

175 **At a talk Ann Coulter was giving at the University of Ottawa:** "Ann Coulter Stirs Controversy in Canada," Rick's List, CNN News, March 24, 2010; transcript at http://bit.ly/HrXHzL.

176 **"I was going to say something about John Edwards":** "Coulter Under Fire for Anti-Gay Slur," CNN.com, March 4, 2007, http://bit.ly/HiQoFZ.

176 **this kind of assholism is close to snark:** David Denby, *Snark* (Simon & Schuster, 2009), p.1.

177 **the South Carolina Democratic chairwoman Carol Fowler on Palin:** Jonathan Martin, "S.C. Dem Chair: Palin Primary Qualification Is She Hasn't Had an Abortion," *Politico,* September 10, 2008, http://politi.co/wUr9e5.

177 **For real satire, listen to the way Bill Maher:** "New Rules," *Real Time with Bill Maher,* HBO, episode 162, July 31, 2009; transcript at http://itsh.bo/A5xmSM.

178 **When Westbrook Pegler referred to Jews as geese:** Diane McWhorter, "Dangerous Minds: Revisiting the Controversial Career of Westbrook Pegler," *Slate,* March 4, 2004, http://slate.me/IrzbvV.

178 **"attempts to micromanage casual conversation":** Excerpts from president's speech to University of Michigan graduates, *New York Times,* May 05, 1995.

179 **As the Irish critic Finian O'Toole wrote:** Finian O'Toole, *Irish Times,* May 5, 1994.

179 **"Mr. Helms, I know this might not be politically correct to say":** Quoted in Cynthia Tucker, "The Not-So-Subtle Code(s) of Racism," *San Francisco Chronicle,* September 18, 1995.

181 **"PC campus administrators":** Charlotte Allen, "War Waged on College Fraternities," *Los Angeles Times,* June 8, 2011.

181 **"spent their time painting murals of their own vaginas"**: "News'View:The Right Kind of Feminism," *Yale Daily News*, October 18, 2010, http://bit.ly/I92hyd.

182 **"A little political correctness never hurt anybody"**: Mike Imrem, "Guillen's Suspension Not Long Enough," *Chicago Herald*, April 10, 2012, http://bit.ly/HBLWmT.

183 **"In a 2011 Rasmussen poll"**: "79% See Political Correctness as Serious Problem in America," Rasmussen Reports, November 2, 2011, http://bit.ly/IhuAut.

184 **Bobby Vinton and Bob Dylan:** Jonathan Leaf, "The Legend of Woodstock Is a Distorted Truth," *Human Events,* August 13, 2009, http://bit.ly/I6i6Uh.

184 **can be said to have begun with** *Beowulf:* Elizabeth Kantor, *The Politically Incorrect Guide to English and American Literature* (Regnery, 2006) p. 3.

184 **We've come to the point:** Conservapedia.com, "Theory of Relativity," http://bit.ly/HtXo7W.

184 **the social psychologist Jonathan Haidt likens:** Interview on *Moyers & Company*, February 12, 2012; text at Truth-Out.org, http://bit.ly/HrxKLo.

185 **There are plenty of comparable things on the left:** Ronald Radosh, "Why Conservatives Are So Upset with Thomas Woods' Politically Incorrect History Book," History News Network, March 6, 2005, http://bit.ly/InK5pg. Michael Kazin, "Howard Zinn's Disappointing History of the United States," History News Network, February 9, 2010, http://bit.ly/Hy46nq.

186 **"No battle for the soul of America rages":** Morris Fiorina, *Culture War?:The Myth of a Polarized America* (Longman, 2004), p. 5.; Morris Fiorina and Samuel J.Abrams, "Political Polarization in the American Public," *Annual Review of Political Science*, June 2008, vol. 11: 563–588.

189 **As one conservative puts it:** "5 Reasons Liberals Aren't as Happy as Conservatives," Rightwing News, http://bit.ly/I2yknP.

189 **A 2009 Pew study:** Aaron Smith, Kay Lehman Schlozman, Sidney Verba, and Henry Brady, "The Current State of Civic Engagement," Pew Internet, September 1, 2009, http://bit.ly/IsbL9D.

190 **it's more unsettling to hear Republican congressmen:** Dana Milbank, "Bush's Bill Suffers a Torturous Day in Committee," *Washington Post*, September 21, 2006.

190 **Conservatives often point to surveys:** "Are We Happy Yet?," Pew Research Center survey, February 16, 2006, http://bit.ly/HvHdok; Dennis Prager, "Why Unhappy People Become Liberals," *National Review* online, November 23, 2010, http://bit.ly/IkIIoW.

191 **As Theda Skocpol and Vanessa Williams note:** Theda Skocpol and Vanessa Williams, *The Tea Party and the Remaking of Republican Conservatism* (Oxford University Press, 2012), p. 128.

192 **conservatives are more densely connected:** In a large-scale statistical analysis of tweets by political candidates during the 2010 midterm elections, a group of University of Michigan researchers found that conservatives in general maintained more consistent content and denser graphs of interconnections. Other researchers have found the same left-right differential in looking at tweets between legislators and constituents. Avishay Livne, Matthew Simmons, Eytan Adar, and Lada A. Admic, "The Party Is Over Here: Structure and Content in the 2010 Election," Proceedings of the Fifth International Conference on Weblogs and Social Media, 2011, Barcelona, Spain, July 17–21, 2011, http://bit.ly/tWaR5C. David Sparks, "Birds of a Feather Tweet Together: Partisan Structure in Online Social Networks," presented at the 68th meeting of the Midwest Political Science Association, 2010, Chicago, Illinois, April 22–25, 2010, http://bit.ly/HnpgWu.

193 **NPR would not be referring to American waterboarding:** "Your Voices Have Been Heard," NPR Ombudsman with Edward Shumacher-Matos, NPR, June 30, 2009, http://n.pr/IjvPvi.

194 **When people are asked:** Among conservatives, standing firm is preferred to compromise by 60 to 34 percent, and among those who say they're very conservative, standing firm is preferred by 72 to 17 percent. Among liberals, compromise is preferred by 59 to 36 percent, and among those identifying themselves as progressives, compromise wins out by 55 to 40 percent. "Nastiness, Name-calling & Negativity," Allegheny College Survey of Civility and Compromise in American Politics, April 20, 2010, http://sites.allegheny.edu/civility/.

195 **It takes the modern right far from a traditional conservatism:** Edmund Burke, Peter J. Stanlis (ed.), *Edmund Burke: Selected Writings and Speeches* (Regnery, 1963), p. 216.

196 **Conservatives may have had both ideological and personal reasons:** Joel Achenbach and Peter Wallsten, "Heading into N.H. primary, GOP Finds Itself Stuck," *Washington Post*, January 7, 2011. "Rove: Trump a 'Joke Candidate,' Part of the 'Nutty Right,'" Fox News, April 16, 201; transcript at http://bit.ly/Ht4vNk.

201 **"Civility equals censorship,"** Rush Limbaugh said: *The Rush Limbaugh Show*, January 13, 2011; transcript at http://bit.ly/IelpdZ.

201 **"I'm all for good manners but this isn't a dinner party":** Paul Krugman, "The Uncivil War," *New York Times*, November 25, 2003.

201 **"Civility is important,"** Sarah Palin says: "Palin: Obama's State of Union Address Full of 'WTF' Moments," *On the Record with Greta Van Susteren*, Fox News, January 26, 2011; transcript at http://fxn.ws/HPs5gI.

201 **"We don't need lectures from uncivil leftists":** *The Rush Limbaugh Show*, January 13, 2011; transcript at http://bit.ly/IelpdZ.

202 **Some Tea Party protestors on Capitol Hill:** Ravi Somaiya, "Tea Party Protesters Call Black and Gay Lawmakers 'Nigger' and 'Faggot,'" Gawker, March 20, 2010, http://gaw.kr/HWp9C4. "Obama Supporters Call Black Republican an 'Uncle Tom N*gger'," Real Clear Politics, October 5, 2011, http://bit.ly/IbrkVU.

203 **In an article on "liberal incivility":** Gene Lalor, "Bristol Palin and Liberal Incivility," *American Conservative Daily*, September 25, 2011, http://bit.ly/I8ZiJr.

204 **The** *Economist* **distinguishes between the rhetoric that's bal-**

listic: M.S., "Nasty Words Toxic v Ballistic Rhetoric," Democracy in America blog, *Economist*, January 14, 2011, http://econ.st/IelzSz.

204 **You don't have to be a semanticist:** Sam Stein, "Mike McCalister, Florida GOP Senate Candidate, Brings Back Second Amendment Remedies," Huffington Post, November 10, 2011, http://huff.to/vr3j8I. Greg Sargent, "Sharron Angle Floated Possibility of Armed Insurrection," Plum Line blog, *Washington Post*, June 15, 2010, http://wapo.st/IoJcqO.

205 **After Joe Biden told a group of union members:** "Top 10 Examples of Liberal Incivility," *Human Events,* September 17, 2011, http://bit.ly/HrWGbd. Noel Sheppard, "Mark Levin Challenges David Gregory to Report Recent Violent Rhetoric from Democrats," NewsBusters, April 09, 2011, http://bit.ly/yT1OdW.

205 **And MSNBC's Ed Schulz goes after Michele Bachmann:** John Hinderaker, "Paul Krugman, Buffoon," *Powerline* blog, January 11, 2011, http://www.powerlineblog.com/archives/2011/01/028118.php.

206 **the editors of the *New Republic* tried to distinguish incivility:** "After Arizona: Incivility, Yes. Indecency, No." *New Republic*, January 12, 2011.

206 **In what had to be the most absurd linguistic overreaction:** Chellie Pingree, "For Gabby's Sake, Republicans Should Change the Name of Their Health Care Repeal Bill," Huffington Post, January 9, 2011, http://huff.to/HEXrLZ.

207 **When Dick Gephardt said:** "RNC Chairman: Democrats Increasingly 'Liberal, Elitist, Angry,'" CNN, December 4, 2003, http://bit.ly/IgW2uG.

209 **David Axelrod describes a Romney campaign strategy:** "RJC Denounces Axelrod's 'Mittzkrieg' Comment, Calls On Democrats to Do the Same," Republican Jewish Coalition, March 19, 2012, http://bit.ly/HJn7Fo.

211 **"But when the object of his mockery":** Immanuel Kant, "The Metaphysical Principles of Virtue," in *Ethical Philosophy,* trans. James W. Ellington (Indianapolis: Hackett, 1983), p. 127.

A Note on the Figures

229 **"The figures used in this book were drawn from the ngrams tool":** Jean-Baptiste Michel et al., "Quantitative analysis of culture using millions of digitized books," *Science*, January 14, 2011, pp. 176–183.

229 **"a considerable number of books in the Google Books are misdated":** Geoffrey Nunberg, "Google's Book Search: A Disaster for Scholars," *The Chronicle of Higher Education Review*, August 31, 2009, http://bit.ly/mT18YB; response by Jon Orwant of Google at Language Log, http://bit.ly/H55iDu.

Acknowledgments

One of the things that makes the notion of the asshole both fascinating and daunting is that its trail winds through many different territories: from country music to feminism, from Trilling to Trump, from *The Naked and the Dead* to *Animal House*. I haven't tried to achieve a synthesis here; I was more interested in following the word wherever it took me, with the idea that the breadth of the itinerary alone would make the point. But I would have lost my way more often if I didn't have a lot of guides to help me. Over the course of writing the book, I turned again and again to Rachel Brownstein, Paul Duguid, Kathleen Miller, and Bob Newsom. They, along with Bob Asahina, Todd Gitlin, and Barbara Nunberg, took the time to read parts of the manuscript and give me useful comments. For advice and background on various and sundry, I was fortunate to be able to pick the brains of Leo Braudy, David Henkin, Richard Hardack, Mark Liberman, Sophie Nunberg, Scott Parker, and Tom Wasow. For observations about the use of *asshole* in particular English varieties or about equivalent words in other languages, I'm grateful to Francesco Antinucci, John Rickford, Francisco Hulse, François Recanati, Hinrich Schuetze, Jesse Sheidlower, Arthur Spear, Annie Zaenen, and Jonathan Lighter (from whose magisterial *Historical Dictionary of American Slang* I drew numerous observations about the history of these words). I learned a lot, too, from the comments I received when I gave talks on some of this material at Stanford University, the Yale Humanities Center, the University of Massachusetts, the Townsend Center for the Humanities at Berkeley, the Berkeley Cognitive Science Group, the Frank Institute for the Humanities at the University of Chicago, and the Institut Jean Nicod in Paris. Thanks to Dan Perkel, who did a lot of work converting the figures to a publishable form and extracting clean endnotes from a very messy manuscript. And thanks as always to my agent Joe Spieler and to Clive Priddle, my editor at PublicAffairs, both of whom were called on to be especially patient with this one.

Given the topic of this book, a formal dedication might be misconstrued. But I wouldn't have been able to finish it without the loving support of my wife, Kathleen Miller. For that and many other things, I owe her more than I can say.

A Note on the Figures

The figures used in this book were drawn from the ngrams tool developed by Google Labs (http://books.google.com/ngrams/), which plots yearly changes in the relative frequency of terms in a set of about five million books drawn from the Google Books corpus, the English-language portion of which contains about 360 billion words in all. For each term and each publication year, the tool computes what proportion the term represents of the words in all the books published in that year, up to the year 2000. As presented here, the graphs show, not the absolute frequencies of these words, but the rates of increasing or decreasing frequency over time. The important thing is the slope of the curve, not its height. Figure 4.1, for example, does not indicate that *lifestyle* and *trendy* are equal in frequency—in fact *lifestyle* is far more common—but rather that they entered everyday usage at about the same time and increased in frequency at the same rate.

There are several limits to this tool. First, a considerable number of books in the Google Books are misdated or contain other inaccurate metadata, though the problems are somewhat less serious in the ngrams corpus than in the Google Books corpus as a whole, and don't substantially alter the results of these searches. Second, it should be borne in mind that the frequency of terms in published books doesn't necessarily correlate with their frequency in the spoken language, particularly when it comes to vulgar words like *asshole*. There's no question that a part of the increase in frequency of that word in the Google Books corpus reflects only the increasing willingness of publishers to print it, particularly in the 1950s and 1960s.

Asshole presents a further problem, moreover, in having both anatomical and figurative uses. But, we can sort these uses out by comparing the results of searches on phrases like *your asshole*, which return almost exclusively anatomical uses, with searches on phrases like *you asshole,* which return almost exclusively uses of the word as an insult.* (The plural *assholes* and the phrase *an asshole* are similar to *you asshole*; any of these can be taken as a good proxy for the overall frequency of the figurative use of the word.) That in turn enables us to factor out the effects of the relaxation of taboos on printing the word. As the following figure shows, between 1950 and 1975 the frequencies of the two uses increased more or less in tandem. But from then on the anatomical use leveled off, while the figurative use continued to climb. By the mid-1990s it had become several times more frequent than the anatomical use, which could only reflect the increasing popularity of this particular use of the word, not the increasing acceptability of printing it. (Note that unlike the other figures in the book, this one presents the absolute frequency of both expressions, since that is what matters here.)

---

*Searches on *your asshole* return a few instances of phrases like *your asshole friend*, but more than 99 percent of the hits are anatomical.

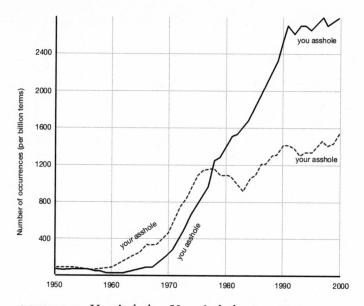

FIGURE A-I. You Asshole v. Your Asshole, 1950–2000

Index

About the Author

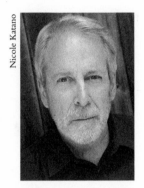

Geoffrey Nunberg, a linguist, is a professor at the UC Berkeley School of Information. Since 1987, he has done a language feature on NPR's "Fresh Air," and his commentaries have appeared in the *New York Times* and many other publications. He is the emeritus chair of the Usage Panel of the *American Heritage Dictionary* and a winner of the Linguistic Society of America's Language and the Public Interest Award. His previous books include *Talking Right* and *Going Nucular.* Nunberg lives in San Francisco.

PUBLICAFFAIRS is a publishing house founded in 1997. It is a tribute to the standards, values, and flair of three persons who have served as mentors to countless reporters, writers, editors, and book people of all kinds, including me.

I. F. STONE, proprietor of *I. F. Stone's Weekly,* combined a commitment to the First Amendment with entrepreneurial zeal and reporting skill and became one of the great independent journalists in American history. At the age of eighty, Izzy published *The Trial of Socrates,* which was a national bestseller. He wrote the book after he taught himself ancient Greek.

BENJAMIN C. BRADLEE was for nearly thirty years the charismatic editorial leader of *The Washington Post.* It was Ben who gave the *Post* the range and courage to pursue such historic issues as Watergate. He supported his reporters with a tenacity that made them fearless, and it is no accident that so many became authors of influential, bestselling books.

ROBERT L. BERNSTEIN, the chief executive of Random House for more than a quarter century, guided one of the nation's premier publishing houses. Bob was personally responsible for many books of political dissent and argument that challenged tyranny around the globe. He is also the founder and was the longtime chair of Human Rights Watch, one of the most respected human rights organizations in the world.

．　．　．

For fifty years, the banner of Public Affairs Press was carried by its owner Morris B. Schnapper, who published Gandhi, Nasser, Toynbee, Truman, and about 1,500 other authors. In 1983 Schnapper was described by *The Washington Post* as "a redoubtable gadfly." His legacy will endure in the books to come.

Peter Osnos, *Founder and Editor-at-Large*